I0013247

Disclaimer: The information contained in this book is for educational purposes only. While every effort has been made to ensure the accuracy of the content, the author and publisher disclaim any responsibility for errors or omissions. Readers are encouraged to seek professional advice where needed.

Kotlin for

AR

Practical Projects for Building Stunning
Augmented Reality Apps on Android

BY

A.L Grey

Contents

7

Preface

Why Kotlin and AR Are the Perfect Pair

Welcome to the exciting world of Augmented Reality (AR) development with Kotlin! If you're here, you're probably curious about creating innovative, immersive experiences on Android devices. Let me tell you—you've made an excellent choice. Kotlin and AR go together like a finely tuned symphony, delivering a perfect blend of simplicity, power, and modern design that makes AR development accessible and rewarding.

Kotlin, officially supported by Google for Android development, has quickly become the go-to language for developers worldwide. Why? Because it simplifies coding while enhancing functionality, making it ideal for handling the complexities of AR. On the other hand, AR has redefined how we interact with technology, blending the digital and physical worlds seamlessly. From gaming and education to retail and healthcare, AR is revolutionizing industries, and Kotlin provides the tools to create engaging apps to thrive in this space.

How to Use This Book

This book is designed to take you step by step into the world of AR development using Kotlin. Whether you're a beginner looking to start your journey or an experienced developer aiming to explore AR, this book has something for everyone.

Here's how you can make the most of it:

- **Follow Along with Hands-On Projects**: Every chapter includes a practical project to apply what you learn. For instance, when we discuss ARCore, you'll build an app that places 3D objects in the real world. These projects ensure you're not just reading—you're building as you go.

- **Learn Concepts Gradually**: The chapters progress from foundational knowledge to advanced techniques. If you're new to AR or Kotlin, start from the beginning and work your way through. If you're already familiar with the basics, feel free to skip ahead.
- **Experiment and Explore**: While the examples provided are detailed, don't hesitate to tweak them. Try out your own ideas to see how ARCore and Kotlin respond. AR development thrives on creativity.
- **Leverage Resources**: In the appendices, you'll find cheat sheets, troubleshooting guides, and references to keep handy as you develop.

Prerequisites and Setup

Before diving in, let's ensure you're equipped with the tools and knowledge needed for a smooth experience:

1. **Basic Programming Knowledge**: A familiarity with any programming language is helpful, though not mandatory. If you've worked with Java or Kotlin before, even better!
2. **A Computer with the Following Setup**:
    - **Operating System**: Windows, macOS, or Linux.
    - **Android Studio Installed**: This is the primary IDE we'll use. Download the latest version from the official site.
    - **Kotlin Plugin**: Android Studio includes built-in support for Kotlin, but ensure it's up to date.
3. **A Compatible Android Device**:
    - ARCore-compatible Android phone or tablet. You can check

12

compatibility on Google's ARCore support page.

4. **Google Play Services for AR**:
   - Install the "Google Play Services for AR" app from the Play Store on your device.

5. **A Creative Mindset**: AR development is as much about imagination as it is about coding. You'll be creating experiences that blur the line between the digital and physical worlds, so think outside the box!

Why This Book Stands Out

Throughout this journey, you'll notice a focus on clarity, practicality, and innovation. Unlike traditional programming guides that may overwhelm with jargon, this book is conversational and approachable. Think of me as your friendly guide, walking with you through the fascinating world of AR.

Each concept is paired with real-world examples and practical projects that mirror scenarios you'll encounter in app development. For example, when learning about ARCore's motion tracking, you'll build an app to detect and respond to real-world movement—an essential feature in modern AR applications.

By the end of this book, you won't just understand the *how* of AR development— you'll understand the *why*. You'll have the confidence to not only follow tutorials but also create your own unique AR experiences that stand out in a competitive market.

So, are you ready to turn your ideas into reality? Let's get started!

Chapter 1: Introduction to Augmented Reality

1.1 What is Augmented Reality?

Augmented Reality (AR) is a fascinating technology that enhances the real world by overlaying digital content, such as images, sounds, or 3D models, onto your physical surroundings. Unlike Virtual Reality (VR), which immerses users in a completely virtual environment, AR enriches your view of the real world by combining it with digital elements in real-time.

Let's break this down. Think of AR as a way for your device to "understand" the world around you and project interactive visuals onto it. Whether you're catching Pokémon in **Pokémon GO** or visualizing how a piece of furniture looks in your living room before buying it, AR is the technology behind these immersive experiences.

How AR Works

At its core, AR relies on three fundamental components:

1. **Device Hardware**: Cameras, motion sensors (gyroscopes and accelerometers), and processors in your phone or tablet help capture and analyze the environment.
2. **Software Frameworks**: Platforms like ARCore (Google's AR SDK) enable AR capabilities by providing tools for motion tracking, surface detection, and light estimation.
3. **Digital Content**: This is the virtual information (e.g., 3D objects or annotations) rendered over the physical world. AR ensures this content is context-aware and aligned with real-world objects.

Real-World Applications of AR

AR isn't just for entertainment—it's transforming industries in meaningful ways:

- **Education**: AR apps like Google Expeditions allow students to explore historical landmarks or human anatomy interactively.
- **Retail**: IKEA's app lets you place virtual furniture in your home to see how it fits.
- **Healthcare**: Surgeons use AR for detailed 3D visualization of a patient's anatomy during procedures.
- **Gaming and Entertainment**: Games like Pokémon GO or social media filters that add masks or effects to your selfies.

These examples show that AR is not a futuristic concept—it's happening now, and developers like you are the key to its evolution.

1.2 Key AR Concepts: ARCore, Anchors, and Sessions

Understanding AR development begins with mastering three foundational concepts: **ARCore**, **Anchors**, and **Sessions**. These components work together to make augmented reality possible, enabling virtual objects to interact seamlessly with the physical world.

ARCore: The Backbone of AR on Android

ARCore is Google's software development kit (SDK) that brings AR capabilities to Android devices. It provides essential tools for creating AR apps by leveraging the device's camera, motion sensors, and advanced algorithms.

Core Features of ARCore:

1. **Motion Tracking:** ARCore uses the device's camera to understand how it moves through the environment. This keeps virtual objects stable and correctly positioned as you move.
2. **Environmental Understanding:** It detects flat surfaces (planes) like tables, floors, or walls, allowing developers to anchor objects in real-world spaces.
3. **Light Estimation:** ARCore analyzes the ambient light to adjust the brightness and shadows of virtual objects, making them appear more realistic.

Key ARCore Classes:

- `ArFragment`: A simplified entry point for building AR experiences.
- `Plane`: Represents detected flat surfaces.

- **Anchor**: Links virtual objects to specific points in the real world.

Anchors: Fixing Virtual Objects in the Real World

In AR, an **Anchor** is a reference point that ties virtual objects to specific positions in the physical environment. Without anchors, objects would "float" as you move your device, breaking the illusion of AR.

Here's how anchors work:

- When ARCore detects a plane, you can place an anchor on it. This anchor ensures that the object remains fixed to that spot, even as you walk around or change your viewing angle.
- An anchor's position is updated continuously based on the device's motion tracking, keeping it stable in the scene.

Example Code: Placing an Anchor Let's look at a snippet to place an anchor on a detected plane:

kotlin

```
arFragment.setOnTapArPlaneLis
tener  {  hitResult,  plane,
motionEvent ->

    // Create  an  anchor  at
the tap location

    val       anchor        =
hitResult.createAnchor()



    // Attach  a  3D  model  to
the  anchor  (model  setup  is
shown later)

    placeObject(anchor)

}
```

This snippet ensures that whenever the user taps a plane, an anchor is created, and a virtual object is attached.

Sessions: Managing AR Data Over Time

An **AR Session** is the engine that drives ARCore. It acts as the control center, managing all the information about the environment and the device's position over time.

Key Responsibilities of an AR Session:

1. **Tracking:** Continuously monitors the device's position relative to the environment.
2. **Plane Detection:** Scans for and identifies flat surfaces where objects can be placed.
3. **Environmental Updates:** Dynamically updates the environment map as the user moves.

Think of a session as a "timeline" for your AR experience, starting when the app launches and running until the app is closed. During this time, the session ensures the AR environment stays consistent.

Example Code: Configuring an AR Session Here's a basic configuration for an AR session in Kotlin:

kotlin

```
val         arSession        =
Session(this).apply {

    // Enable plane detection

    val        config        =
Config(this).apply {

        planeFindingMode     =
Config.PlaneFindingMode.HORIZ
ONTAL_AND_VERTICAL
```

```
    }

    configure(config)

}
```

In this example:

- We enable both horizontal and vertical plane detection.
- The session uses this configuration to detect surfaces and track motion.

Bringing It All Together

To see ARCore, anchors, and sessions in action, here's a complete workflow example:

1. **Detect a Plane**
   ARCore scans the environment and identifies a horizontal plane.
2. **Place an Anchor**
   When the user taps the screen, an

anchor is created at the point of interaction.

3. **Attach a Virtual Object**
A 3D object is rendered at the anchor's location, fixed in the real-world position.

Here's a practical example combining these steps:

kotlin

```
arFragment.setOnTapArPlaneLis
tener { hitResult, plane,
motionEvent ->

    // Create an anchor

    val anchor =
hitResult.createAnchor()
```

```kotlin
// Build and render a 3D
model

ModelRenderable.builder()

    .setSource(this,
R.raw.simple_cube)

    .build()

    .thenAccept            {
modelRenderable ->

        val anchorNode  =
AnchorNode(anchor).apply {


setParent(arFragment.arSceneV
iew.scene)

        }

        val
transformableNode            =
```

```
TransformableNode(arFragment.
transformationSystem).apply {


setParent(anchorNode)

                renderable    =
modelRenderable

            }

        }

}
```

1.3 How AR is Changing Mobile Development

Augmented Reality (AR) has redefined what mobile devices are capable of, transforming them from mere communication tools into gateways to immersive experiences. By

27

blending the digital and physical worlds, AR is reshaping the landscape of mobile development across industries, inspiring new use cases, enhancing user engagement, and opening up exciting opportunities for developers.

Key Areas Where AR is Impacting Mobile Development

1. **Enhanced User Interaction**
   AR introduces a new layer of interaction that feels natural and intuitive. Instead of merely touching a screen, users can now interact with digital objects in the real world. Apps like Snapchat, with its AR filters, and Google Lens, which provides real-time information through your camera, are great examples of AR's potential to make user experiences more immersive.

2. **Gamification and Engagement**
   AR has revolutionized mobile

gaming. Games like **Pokémon GO** and **Harry Potter: Wizards Unite** showcase how AR can create deeply engaging experiences by merging gameplay with real-world locations. This kind of interaction fosters user retention and viral growth.

3. **Real-World Applications**
   AR is no longer just about entertainment. It's driving innovation in various industries:
   - **Retail**: Apps like IKEA Place allow users to visualize furniture in their homes before purchasing.
   - **Education**: Tools like Google Expeditions AR make learning interactive by bringing concepts to life in 3D.
   - **Healthcare**: AR aids surgeons with real-time visualization of anatomy during complex procedures.

Challenges AR Solves in Mobile Development

1. **Bridging the Gap Between Physical and Digital**
   AR allows developers to create apps that provide real-time, context-aware solutions. For example:
   - **Navigation Apps**: Google Maps' Live View overlays walking directions directly onto the user's environment.
   - **Repair Guides**: Apps can overlay step-by-step instructions on machinery, guiding users through repairs.
2. **Improved Personalization**
   By understanding and mapping the environment, AR apps can tailor content to a user's surroundings, creating unique, personalized experiences.
3. **Data Visualization**
   AR makes complex data more digestible by representing it in 3D space. For instance, AR apps in

30

architecture and design can render building layouts in real-world settings.

How AR Influences Mobile Development Practices

1. **New Design Paradigms**
   Designing AR experiences requires thinking beyond flat interfaces. Developers must consider spatial design, focusing on:
   - **Depth and Scale**: Objects must be realistic in size and positioning.
   - **Lighting and Shadows**: Proper light estimation ensures objects blend naturally with their environment.
2. **Optimizing Performance**
   AR apps require significant computational power. Developers must optimize for:

- Efficient rendering to prevent lag or crashes.
- Battery and CPU usage to ensure devices don't overheat during extended sessions.

Practical Example: Enhancing a Retail App with AR

Let's create a feature that allows users to visualize products in their homes. Imagine an app for placing virtual furniture in a room.

Step 1: Detecting a Surface
Use ARCore's plane detection to identify a flat surface:

kotlin

```
arFragment.setOnTapArPlaneLis
tener   {   hitResult,   plane,
motionEvent ->
```

```kotlin
    if      (plane.type      ==
Plane.Type.HORIZONTAL_UPWARD_
FACING) {

        val      anchor      =
hitResult.createAnchor()

        placeObject(anchor)

    }

}
```

Step 2: Rendering a Virtual Object
Attach a virtual chair model to the detected
anchor:

kotlin

```kotlin
private                      fun
placeObject(anchor: Anchor) {

    ModelRenderable.builder()
```

```kotlin
        .setSource(this,
R.raw.chair_model) // Ensure
the chair model is in your
resources

        .build()

        .thenAccept            {
modelRenderable ->

            val anchorNode =
AnchorNode(anchor).apply {


setParent(arFragment.arSceneV
iew.scene)

                }


TransformableNode(arFragment.
transformationSystem).apply {

setParent(anchorNode)
```

```
                    renderable   =
modelRenderable

                    }

          }

}
```

When the user taps on a detected plane, the app places the chair model there, and they can scale or rotate it to see how it fits into their space.

The Future of AR in Mobile Development

1. **5G and Edge Computing**
   The rollout of 5G networks significantly enhances AR's potential, enabling faster data transfer and reduced latency. This makes real-time AR experiences smoother and more accessible.

2. **AI Integration**
   Combining AR with AI takes it to the
   next level. For instance:
   - ○ AI can recognize objects in a
     user's environment and provide
     relevant AR overlays.
   - ○ AR apps can predict user
     behavior to make interactions
     more seamless.
3. **Cross-Platform Development**
   Tools like Unity and Unreal Engine
   simplify AR development for both
   Android and iOS, encouraging
   developers to create AR apps that
   reach a broader audience.

1.4 Understanding Kotlin: A Quick Overview for Beginners

Kotlin is a modern, concise, and powerful
programming language developed by
JetBrains. Officially supported by Google as
the preferred language for Android
development, Kotlin has gained immense

popularity for its ease of use, safety features, and seamless interoperability with Java. In this section, we'll provide a clear, beginner-friendly overview of Kotlin, highlighting the concepts and features that make it an excellent choice for AR development.

Why Learn Kotlin?

Kotlin simplifies Android development by reducing boilerplate code, enhancing readability, and providing robust tools for error handling. Its expressive syntax and modern features make it beginner-friendly yet powerful enough for advanced applications like augmented reality.

Getting Started with Kotlin: The Basics

Declaring   **Variables**
In Kotlin, variables can be declared as either mutable (`var`) or immutable (`val`). kotlin

37

```
val    name    =    "Kotlin"    //
Immutable    variable    (read-
only)

var  age  =  5              //
Mutable variable

age  =  6                   //
Allowed    because    'age'    is
mutable
```

1.

Type   **Inference**
Kotlin is smart enough to infer the type of a
variable, so you don't always need to
specify   it.
kotlin

```
val  language  =  "Kotlin"  //
Kotlin    infers    this    is    a
String
```

```kotlin
var version = 1.8          // Inferred as Double
```

2.

Functions

Functions in Kotlin are simple and concise, and they can have default arguments.
kotlin

```kotlin
fun greet(name: String = "World"): String {

    return "Hello, $name!"

}
```

```kotlin
println(greet())           // Output: Hello, World!

println(greet("Kotlin"))   // Output: Hello, Kotlin!
```

3.

Key Features of Kotlin

Null **Safety**
Kotlin reduces the chances of `NullPointerException` by distinguishing between nullable and non-nullable types.
kotlin

```
var nonNullable: String = "Hello"

var nullable: String? = null



// Safe call operator (?.)
prevents null pointer
exceptions
```

```kotlin
println(nullable?.length)    //
Output: null
```

1.

Interoperability   with   Java
Kotlin can seamlessly call Java code and
vice versa. This makes it easy to integrate
Kotlin   into   existing   projects.
java

```java
// Java code

public class JavaClass {

    public String greet() {

        return   "Hello   from
Java!";

    }

}
```

kotlin

```kotlin
// Kotlin code

val javaClass = JavaClass()

println(javaClass.greet())  //
Output: Hello from Java!
```

Extension Functions
Kotlin allows you to add new functions to
existing classes without modifying them.
kotlin

```kotlin
fun String.isPalindrome():
Boolean {

    return       this       ==
this.reversed()

}
```

```kotlin
println("level".isPalindrome(
)) // Output: true
```

Practical Example: A Simple Kotlin App

Let's write a simple Kotlin program that demonstrates basic concepts like variables, loops, and functions.

Goal: Calculate the sum of all even numbers up to a given number.

kotlin

```kotlin
fun main() {

    println("Enter        a
number:")
```

```kotlin
    val         number         =
readLine()?.toIntOrNull()    ?:
0 // Read user input safely


    println("Sum       of     even
numbers     up     to     $number:
${sumOfEvenNumbers(number)}")

}


fun    sumOfEvenNumbers(limit:
Int): Int {

    var sum = 0

    for (i in 1..limit) { //
Loop    from    1    to    the    given
number

        if (i % 2 == 0) { //
Check if the number is even
```

```
            sum += i

        }

    }

    return sum

}
```

Output:

mathematica

```
Enter a number:

10

Sum of even numbers up to 10:
30
```

Kotlin for Android: Why It's a Game-Changer

Concise   **Code**

Kotlin's syntax is designed to minimize boilerplate code. For example, here's how to set a click listener in Java vs. Kotlin:

Java:

java

```
button.setOnClickListener(new
View.OnClickListener() {

    @Override

    public void onClick(View
v) {

        // Do something

    }

});
```

Kotlin:

kotlin

```kotlin
button.setOnClickListener {

    // Do something

}
```

Coroutines for Asynchronous Programming

Kotlin's coroutines make managing background tasks like network calls simple and efficient.

kotlin

```kotlin
GlobalScope.launch {

    val      result      =
fetchDataFromServer()

    println("Data     received:
$result")
```

```
}


suspend                    fun
fetchDataFromServer():  String
{

    delay(1000) // Simulate a
network delay

    return "Hello, AR World!"

}
```

Building Confidence with Kotlin

To build proficiency, start with small
projects, like a calculator app or a to-do list.
Use online Kotlin playgrounds (like
play.kotlinlang.org) for experimentation and
practice.

48

Kotlin's simplicity, modern features, and compatibility with Java make it an excellent choice for both beginners and experienced developers. Whether you're building simple apps or advanced AR experiences, Kotlin equips you with the tools to create efficient, elegant, and robust applications.

1.5 Why Kotlin is Ideal for AR Development

Kotlin has established itself as a top choice for Android development, and when it comes to augmented reality (AR), it shines even brighter. Its modern features, simplicity, and compatibility with Android development tools make Kotlin an excellent match for the challenges and opportunities in AR development. Let's dive into why Kotlin stands out as the language of choice for crafting immersive AR experiences.

1. Simplicity and Conciseness

Kotlin's expressive syntax allows developers to write clean, readable, and concise code. This is especially important in AR development, where maintaining clarity in complex spatial calculations and event handling is essential.

Example: Setting up a click listener in Kotlin

kotlin

```
button.setOnClickListener {
    println("Button
clicked!")
}
```

Compared to Java, Kotlin reduces boilerplate code, enabling you to focus more on building functionality rather than managing repetitive tasks.

2. Null Safety: Avoiding Common Errors

In AR development, handling real-world inputs like device sensors and user interactions can lead to unexpected null values. Kotlin's built-in null safety features prevent crashes caused by null references, ensuring a smoother user experience.

Example: Handling nullable types

kotlin

```
val userInput: String? = null
// Nullable type
val          length          =
userInput?.length ?: 0 //
Safe call with default value
println("Length: $length") //
Output: Length: 0
```

In AR applications, where data from sensors or external sources might be unreliable, this feature provides extra robustness.

---

3. Seamless Interoperability with Java

If you're building an AR app, you may need to integrate with existing Java libraries or frameworks, such as ARCore or third-party AR SDKs. Kotlin's interoperability ensures that you can use these libraries without any hassle, allowing you to leverage the best of both worlds.

Example: Using ARCore's Java-based API in Kotlin

kotlin

```
val session = Session(this)
// ARCore session
initialization
val config =
Config(session).apply {
```

```
    focusMode                =
Config.FocusMode.AUTO
}
session.configure(config)
```

This seamless compatibility enables developers to adopt Kotlin gradually in AR projects while still utilizing Java-based tools.

---

4. Advanced Features for AR Development

AR development often involves handling asynchronous tasks like downloading 3D models, processing sensor data, or running complex calculations. Kotlin provides tools like **coroutines** to simplify and optimize such workflows.

Example: Using coroutines for asynchronous tasks

kotlin

```kotlin
GlobalScope.launch {
    val model = load3DModel()
// Simulate loading a 3D
model
    println("Model      loaded:
$model")
}

suspend    fun    load3DModel():
String {
    delay(2000)   // Simulate
network delay
    return "3D Model Data"
}
```

With coroutines, you can manage background tasks efficiently, keeping the app responsive and ensuring smooth AR interactions.

5. Enhanced Tooling and Community Support

Kotlin is officially supported by Google and integrated into Android Studio, the go-to IDE for Android development. Features like smart code completion, debugging tools, and built-in templates speed up the AR app development process.

Additionally, the Kotlin community is active and growing, offering a wealth of tutorials, libraries, and resources that can simplify complex AR challenges.

6. Kotlin's Suitability for Modern AR Frameworks

ARCore, Google's platform for building AR experiences, pairs naturally with Kotlin. ARCore requires developers to manage complex tasks like detecting planes, tracking objects, and rendering 3D models. Kotlin's concise and expressive syntax makes these tasks easier to implement and maintain.

Example: Using ARCore with Kotlin to detect planes

kotlin

```kotlin
arFragment.setOnTapArPlaneLis
tener  {  hitResult,  plane,
motionEvent ->
    if    (plane.type    ==
Plane.Type.HORIZONTAL_UPWARD_
FACING) {
        val    anchor    =
hitResult.createAnchor()
        placeObject(anchor)
    }
}

fun       placeObject(anchor:
Anchor) {
    ModelRenderable.builder()
        .setSource(this,
R.raw.virtual_object) // Load
a 3D model
```

```
        .build()
        .thenAccept { model -
>
        val anchorNode =
AnchorNode(anchor).apply {

setParent(arFragment.arSceneV
iew.scene)
            }

TransformableNode(arFragment.
transformationSystem).apply {

setParent(anchorNode)
                renderable =
model
            }
        }
}
```

In just a few lines of Kotlin code, you can set up an AR interaction where users tap on detected surfaces to place 3D objects.

---

7. Developer-Friendly Language Design

Kotlin's focus on developer productivity and modern programming practices makes it easier to debug, test, and maintain AR applications. Features like extension functions and data classes help streamline common tasks.

Example: Simplifying a data model with Kotlin

kotlin

```
data class ARObject(val name:
String, val x: Float, val y:
Float, val z: Float)
```

```
val        objectData        =
ARObject("Tree",  1.2f,  3.4f,
5.6f)
println(objectData)        //
Output:    ARObject(name=Tree,
x=1.2, y=3.4, z=5.6)
```

This reduces the boilerplate typically required for such tasks in other languages.

---

8. Future-Ready Development

With the rise of 5G and edge computing, AR applications are becoming more sophisticated, requiring languages and tools that can keep pace with evolving demands. Kotlin's continual updates and alignment with Android's roadmap ensure it remains a future-ready choice for AR development.

Hands-On Project:

Explore ARCore's "Hello AR" Demo and Learn How AR Works.

This hands-on project is designed to give you a solid foundation in building augmented reality (AR) applications using ARCore, Google's platform for AR development. We'll explore the "Hello AR" demo, understand its components, and customize it to build your first AR experience.

What You'll Learn

1. How to set up an ARCore project in Android Studio.
2. The core concepts of ARCore, including session management, plane detection, and anchors.

3. Hands-on coding to create a simple AR app where users can place virtual objects in the real world.

Step 1: Setting Up Your Environment

Prerequisites

1. Install **Android Studio** (latest version).
2. Ensure you have a physical Android device with ARCore support. (Visit ARCore Supported Devices for compatibility.)
3. Install the latest **Java Development Kit (JDK)**.

---

1. Install Required Dependencies

1. Open Android Studio and create a new project. Select the **Empty Activity** template.

Add the following dependencies in your `build.gradle` file to integrate ARCore: gradle

```
dependencies {

    implementation
'com.google.ar:core:1.44.0'
// Ensure the version is up-
to-date

    implementation
'com.google.ar.sceneform:core
:1.17.1'

}
```

2.
3. Sync your project to download the libraries.

Step 2: Configuring the Project

1. Update `AndroidManifest.xml`

Add the required permissions and features
for ARCore:

xml

```
<manifest
xmlns:android="http://schemas
.android.com/apk/res/android"


package="com.example.helloar"
>


    <uses-permission
android:name="android.permiss
ion.CAMERA" />


    <uses-feature
```

```xml
        android:name="android.hardwar
e.camera.ar"

        android:required="true" />


    <application

        android:allowBackup="true"

        android:icon="@mipmap/ic_laun
cher"

        android:label="@string/app_na
me"

        android:theme="@style/Theme.A
ppCompat.Light.NoActionBar">
```

```xml
        <activity
android:name=".MainActivity">

        <intent-filter>

            <action
android:name="android.intent.
action.MAIN" />

            <category
android:name="android.intent.
category.LAUNCHER" />

        </intent-filter>

    </activity>

  </application>

</manifest>
```

2. Create Layout for the AR Experience

In `res/layout/activity_main.xml`, define a container for the AR fragment:

xml

```
<?xml            version="1.0"
encoding="utf-8"?>

<LinearLayout
xmlns:android="http://schemas
.android.com/apk/res/android"


android:layout_width="match_p
arent"


android:layout_height="match_
parent"
```

```xml
android:orientation="vertical
">

    <fragment

android:id="@+id/ar_fragment"

android:name="com.google.ar.s
ceneform.ux.ArFragment"

android:layout_width="match_p
arent"

android:layout_height="match_
parent" />

</LinearLayout>
```

Step 3: Coding the "Hello AR" App

1. Set Up the AR Scene in `MainActivity`

In `MainActivity.kt`, initialize the AR fragment, detect planes, and place virtual objects.

kotlin

```
package com.example.helloar


import android.os.Bundle

import
androidx.appcompat.app.AppCom
patActivity
```

```
import
com.google.ar.core.Anchor

import
com.google.ar.core.Plane

import
com.google.ar.sceneform.Ancho
rNode

import
com.google.ar.sceneform.rende
ring.ModelRenderable

import
com.google.ar.sceneform.ux.Ar
Fragment

import
com.google.ar.sceneform.ux.Tr
ansformableNode
```

```kotlin
class        MainActivity        :
AppCompatActivity() {


    private    lateinit    var
arFragment: ArFragment


    override                fun
onCreate(savedInstanceState:
Bundle?) {

super.onCreate(savedInstanceS
tate)

setContentView(R.layout.activ
ity_main)
```

```kotlin
// Initialize the AR
fragment

arFragment              =
supportFragmentManager.findFr
agmentById(R.id.ar_fragment)
as ArFragment


// Set   up   a   tap
listener for placing objects


arFragment.setOnTapArPlaneLis
tener  {   hitResult,   plane,
motionEvent ->

    if (plane.type ==
Plane.Type.HORIZONTAL_UPWARD_
FACING) {

        val   anchor  =
hitResult.createAnchor()    //
```

```
Create an anchor at the tap
location

placeObject(anchor)

                }

        }

    }


    // Function to place a
virtual object

    private             fun
placeObject(anchor: Anchor) {

        // Load a 3D model


ModelRenderable.builder()
```

```kotlin
            .setSource(this,
R.raw.andy) // Replace with
your 3D model

            .build()

            .thenAccept      {
modelRenderable ->

            // Attach the
model to the anchor

                val
anchorNode                =
AnchorNode(anchor)


anchorNode.setParent(arFragme
nt.arSceneView.scene)


            // Make the
model  transformable  (e.g.,
move, scale, rotate)
```

```kotlin
                val
transformableNode              =
TransformableNode(arFragment.
transformationSystem)


transformableNode.setParent(a
nchorNode)


transformableNode.renderable
= modelRenderable

                }

                .exceptionally   {
throwable ->

                // Handle any
errors loading the model


throwable.printStackTrace()

                null
```

74

```
        }

    }

}
```

Step 4: Add a 3D Model

1. Download a sample 3D model (e.g., a robot or tree) in `.sfb` format.
2. Place the model file (e.g., `andy.sfb`) in the `res/raw` directory of your project.

Step 5: Running the App

1. Connect your ARCore-supported Android device to your computer.
2. Build and run the app on your device using Android Studio.
3. Once the app launches:

- Move your phone around to detect horizontal planes.
- Tap on a plane to place the 3D object.

Understanding How It Works

1. **ARFragment:**
   Manages the AR session and provides an interface for detecting planes and placing objects.
2. **Anchors:**
   Points in the 3D world where virtual objects are placed. They remain fixed even as the user moves around.
3. **Plane Detection:**
   ARCore uses the device's camera to detect horizontal surfaces in the real world.
4. **3D Models:**
   Objects like andy.sfb are rendered in the AR environment, anchored to the detected planes.

Enhancements and Next Steps

1. **Custom Models:**
   Replace andy.sfb with your own 3D models using tools like Blender or download models from repositories like Poly or Sketchfab.
2. **Interaction:**
   Add more interactivity, such as scaling objects or animating them.
3. **Advanced Features:**
   Explore ARCore's capabilities, including lighting estimation, environmental understanding, and persistent anchors.

This hands-on project introduces you to the basics of ARCore and Kotlin, empowering you to create a simple AR app. From detecting planes to placing 3D objects, you now have the foundational knowledge to build more sophisticated AR experiences. In the upcoming chapters, we'll dive deeper into customizing and enhancing AR applications for real-world use cases. Let's keep building!

Chapter 2: Setting Up Your Development Environment

In this chapter, we'll ensure your development environment is fully prepared for AR development with Kotlin and Android. By the end, you'll have Android Studio configured, ARCore set up, and your first Kotlin-based Android AR app running.

2.1 Installing Android Studio and Configuring Kotlin

Developing augmented reality (AR) apps with Kotlin requires a robust and feature-rich development environment. Android Studio, Google's official Integrated Development Environment (IDE) for Android, is perfect for the job. This section will guide you step-by-step through installing Android Studio, configuring it to support Kotlin, and ensuring it is ready for AR development.

Step 1: Downloading Android Studio

1. **Visit the Official Site**
   Open your browser and go to the
   Android Studio download page.
2. **Choose Your Operating System**
   Android Studio supports Windows,
   macOS, and Linux. Select the
   appropriate version for your OS, and
   click **Download.**
3. **Accept the License Agreement**
   Review the terms and conditions, then
   click **Agree and Download** to start
   the download.
4. **Run the Installer**
   Once the file is downloaded, double-
   click it to launch the installer. Follow
   the on-screen instructions:
   - For Windows: Choose the
     installation directory.
   - For macOS: Drag the Android
     Studio icon into the
     Applications folder.

- For Linux: Extract the `.tar.gz` file and run the `studio.sh` script.

Step 2: Setting Up Android Studio

1. **Launch Android Studio**
   Open Android Studio. On the first launch, it may prompt you to import settings from a previous installation. If you're new, select **Do not import settings**.
2. **Complete the Setup Wizard**
   The wizard will guide you through:
   - Downloading the required Android SDK components.
   - Setting up a virtual device (emulator) if desired.
   - Choosing a theme for the IDE (Light or Dark mode).
3. **Verify Installation**
   After completing the setup, you'll see the **Welcome to Android Studio**

screen. This confirms your installation was successful.

Step 3: Enabling Kotlin Support

Android Studio supports Kotlin out of the box, so no additional downloads are needed. However, it's good to ensure the Kotlin plugin is up to date:

1. **Open Plugins Settings**
   - Go to **File > Settings > Plugins** (on Windows/Linux) or **Preferences > Plugins** (on macOS).
2. **Search for Kotlin**
   In the search bar, type **Kotlin**. If the plugin isn't installed or needs an update, click **Install** or **Update**.
3. **Restart Android Studio**
   Once the plugin is installed or updated, restart Android Studio to apply changes.

Step 4: Verifying Kotlin Configuration

To ensure Kotlin is configured correctly, let's create a simple project:

1. **Create a New Project**
   - From the Android Studio welcome screen, click **New Project**.
   - Choose the **Empty Activity** template and click **Next**.
2. **Configure Project Details**
   - Name: `KotlinSetupTest`
   - Package Name: `com.example.kotlindemo`
   - Save Location: Choose a folder on your computer.
   - Language: **Kotlin**
   - Minimum SDK: **API 24: Android 7.0 (Nougat)** or higher.
   - Click **Finish**.
3. **Check the Kotlin Code**

- Open `MainActivity.kt` in the `app/src/main/java` directory.

Replace the default code with: kotlin

```
package
com.example.kotlindemo


import
androidx.appcompat.app.AppCom
patActivity

import android.os.Bundle


class     MainActivity     :
AppCompatActivity() {
```

```kotlin
    override                    fun
onCreate(savedInstanceState:
Bundle?) {

super.onCreate(savedInstanceS
tate)

setContentView(R.layout.activ
ity_main)

    }

}
```

- This is a simple Kotlin program that displays an empty screen.
4. **Run the Project**
    - Connect a physical Android device or use the emulator set up earlier.
    - Click **Run** (green play button) to build and deploy the app.

85

5. **Confirm Success**

   If the app runs without errors and shows an empty screen, your Kotlin setup is working perfectly.

Troubleshooting Tips

- **Installation Errors:**
  Ensure your system meets the minimum requirements for Android Studio.
- **Kotlin Plugin Issues:**
  If you encounter errors with the Kotlin plugin, try reinstalling it from the Plugins settings.
- **Emulator Performance Issues:**
  If the emulator is slow, enable hardware acceleration (HAXM) on Intel-based systems or use a physical device for testing.

Practical Example: A Simple Kotlin Program

To further confirm Kotlin is set up, let's create a small program within Android Studio to print "Hello, Kotlin!" in the log.

Modify `MainActivity.kt`:
kotlin

```
package
com.example.kotlindemo


import
androidx.appcompat.app.AppCom
patActivity

import android.os.Bundle

import android.util.Log
```

```kotlin
class      MainActivity      :
AppCompatActivity() {

    override               fun
onCreate(savedInstanceState:
Bundle?) {

super.onCreate(savedInstanceS
tate)

setContentView(R.layout.activ
ity_main)


    // Log a message

Log.d("KotlinSetupTest",
"Hello, Kotlin!")

    }
```

```
}
```

1.

Run the App and Check Logcat:
Open **Logcat** from the bottom panel in
Android Studio. Filter by
`KotlinSetupTest` to see the message
logged when the app runs.
Output:
makefile

```
D/KotlinSetupTest:      Hello,
Kotlin!
```

2.

2.2 Setting Up ARCore and Android SDK

In this chapter, we'll go through the process
of setting up **ARCore** (Google's AR

framework for Android) along with the necessary **Android SDK** tools. ARCore allows your Android apps to interact with the real world by combining digital content with your physical environment. This is a crucial step for any AR project, and I'll guide you through everything you need to make sure you're ready to build your first AR app.

Step 1: Install the Android SDK

The **Android Software Development Kit (SDK)** is a collection of tools that allows you to develop Android applications. Fortunately, the SDK is bundled with **Android Studio**, so if you've already installed Android Studio, the SDK is already installed. However, we need to make sure everything is up to date to support ARCore development.

1. **Open Android Studio**
   Launch **Android Studio**. If it's your

first time opening it, follow the setup
wizard to configure everything.

2. **Check for SDK Updates**
   - Go to **File > Settings** (on
     Windows/Linux) or **Android
     Studio > Preferences** (on
     macOS).
   - Under **Appearance &
     Behavior > System Settings >
     Android SDK**, you'll see the
     SDK tools available on your
     system. Make sure you have the
     following installed:
     - **Android SDK
       Platform-tools**
     - **Android SDK Build-
       tools**
     - **Android Emulator**
     - **Google Play services**
     - **ARCore SDK**
   - To update the SDK, simply
     check the box next to the tool
     you want to install or update
     and click **Apply**.

3. **SDK Manager**

   The **SDK Manager** is a great place to manage SDK packages. Click on the **SDK Manager** icon in the toolbar (the little icon that looks like a package) to launch the SDK Manager where you can manage and install necessary updates and components.

Step 2: Install ARCore SDK

ARCore is Google's augmented reality SDK that lets you build AR apps for Android. This SDK provides essential tools for working with augmented reality, including features like motion tracking, environmental understanding, and light estimation.

1. **Download the ARCore SDK for Android**
   - Go to the official ARCore SDK page to download the SDK.
   - Alternatively, ARCore is available as a package in the

Google Repository in the **SDK Manager**.

2. **Include ARCore in Your Project**
   To add ARCore to your project, you need to include it as a dependency in your project's build.gradle file.

Open your `app/build.gradle` file, and in the dependencies block, add the ARCore dependency: gradle

```
dependencies {

    implementation
'com.google.ar:core:1.34.0'
// Use the latest version

}
```

   o

You also need to ensure that the **Google Maven repository** is included in your project's `build.gradle`:

gradle

```
allprojects {

    repositories {

        google()    //    Ensure
this line is present

        mavenCentral()

    }

}
```

      ○

3. **Sync the Project**
   After adding the dependency, click
   Sync Now in the yellow notification
   bar at the top of Android Studio to
   sync the project with Gradle.

Step 3: Enable ARCore Features in Your App

For ARCore to work, you need to declare support for AR in your Android app's **manifest file**.

Edit `AndroidManifest.xml`

Open the `AndroidManifest.xml` file located under `app/src/main/`. Add the following permissions and features to declare that your app uses ARCore: xml

```
<uses-permission
android:name="android.permiss
ion.INTERNET" />

<uses-permission
android:name="android.permiss
ion.CAMERA" />


<uses-feature
android:name="android.hardwar
```

```
e.camera"
android:required="true"/>

<uses-feature
android:name="android.hardwar
e.camera.autofocus"
android:required="true"/>

<uses-feature
android:name="android.hardwar
e.sensor.accelerometer"
android:required="true"/>

<uses-feature
android:name="android.hardwar
e.sensor.gyroscope"
android:required="true"/>


<application

    ...>

    <meta-data
```

```
android:name="com.google.ar.c
ore"

        android:value="true"
/>


    . . .

</application>
```

1.

    - ○ This will allow the app to request camera permissions and inform Android that it requires specific hardware features like autofocus, accelerometer, and gyroscope, which are essential for AR.

2. **Testing Your Device's AR Capability**
   ARCore requires specific hardware capabilities. You can check whether your device is compatible with ARCore by installing the **ARCore**

app from the Google Play Store. If your device is compatible, it will work seamlessly with ARCore in your app.

Step 4: Verifying ARCore Installation

To verify that ARCore has been successfully installed and is functioning correctly, let's create a small demo project.

1. **Create a New AR Project**
   If you haven't already, create a new Android project in Android Studio, ensuring that you select **Kotlin** as the language.
2. **Add ARCore to Your Project**
   Open your `build.gradle` (app-level) file and add the ARCore dependency as discussed earlier.

Create a Simple AR Activity
Open the `MainActivity.kt` file and replace the default content with the

following code to initialize ARCore and set up a simple AR session:
kotlin

```
package
com.example.arcoredemo


import android.os.Bundle

import
androidx.appcompat.app.AppCom
patActivity

import
com.google.ar.core.Anchor

import
com.google.ar.core.TrackingSt
ate

import
com.google.ar.session.ArSessi
on
```

```kotlin
class MainActivity :
AppCompatActivity() {

    private lateinit var
arSession: ArSession


    override fun
onCreate(savedInstanceState:
Bundle?) {


super.onCreate(savedInstanceS
tate)


setContentView(R.layout.activ
ity_main)
```

```kotlin
        // Initialize   AR
session

        arSession           =
ArSession(this)

    }


    override fun onResume() {

        super.onResume()

        if
(arSession.isPaused) {

arSession.resume()

        }

    }
```

```
override fun onPause() {

    super.onPause()

    arSession.pause()

    }

}
```

3. This simple activity initializes the AR session when the app starts, resuming it when the app comes to the foreground and pausing it when the app goes into the background.
4. **Test the App**
   Run your app on an AR-compatible device. If everything is set up correctly, you should see ARCore in action once the app starts.

Step 5: Troubleshooting ARCore Setup

If you encounter any issues while setting up ARCore, here are some troubleshooting tips:

- **ARCore Version Mismatch:**
  Always ensure that you are using the latest ARCore version compatible with your Android Studio setup. If you have a mismatch between versions, your app may fail to load ARCore features.
- **Device Compatibility:**
  ARCore only works on devices that meet certain hardware requirements, including a camera, accelerometer, and gyroscope. You can check the ARCore supported devices list to ensure your device is compatible.
- **Permissions Issues:**
  If your app fails to run or crashes when accessing the camera, ensure that you have requested the necessary camera permissions in your **AndroidManifest.xml** and at runtime.

2.3 Creating Your First Android Project for AR

Now that you've set up your development environment and installed the necessary tools like **Android Studio** and **ARCore**, it's time to dive into creating your very first **AR Android app**. In this chapter, we'll walk through the process of creating a basic AR app using **Kotlin** and **ARCore**. Don't worry if you're new to AR development or Android Studio; I'll guide you through every step with clear explanations and hands-on examples.

Step 1: Start a New Android Project

Let's begin by creating a new project in Android Studio.

1. **Open Android Studio**
   If Android Studio is not already open, launch it.
2. **Create a New Project**

- On the welcome screen, click **Start a new Android Studio project**.
- In the **Select a Project Template** window, choose the **Empty Activity** template. This will give you a clean slate for your app.
- Click **Next**.

3. **Configure Your Project**

Now, we need to configure your new project.

- **Name**: Enter the name of your project (e.g., "ARDemo").
- **Package name**: This will be auto-generated, but you can modify it if needed.
- **Save location**: Choose where you want to save your project.
- **Language**: Select **Kotlin** (this is the language we will be using).
- **Minimum API Level**: Choose API level **24 (Android 7.0)** or

higher, as ARCore requires a minimum of API 24.

- ○ Click **Finish**.

Once the project is created, Android Studio will open your project files.

Step 2: Set Up Your Gradle Files

Before we start writing code, we need to add ARCore as a dependency and set up some necessary configurations.

Add   ARCore   Dependency
Open the `build.gradle (Module: app)` file and ensure the following dependency is added to the `dependencies` block:
gradle

```
dependencies {

    implementation
'com.google.ar:core:1.34.0'
// Always use the latest
version of ARCore

}
```

1.
2. **Sync Gradle**
   Once you've added the dependency,
   click **Sync Now** in the yellow bar at
   the top of the editor. This will sync
   your project with the necessary
   dependencies.

Add ARCore Permissions in the Manifest
Open your **AndroidManifest.xml** file and
add the required permissions for ARCore
and the camera:
xml

```
<uses-permission
```

```xml
android:name="android.permiss
ion.INTERNET" />

<uses-permission
android:name="android.permiss
ion.CAMERA" />


<uses-feature
android:name="android.hardwar
e.camera"
android:required="true"/>

<uses-feature
android:name="android.hardwar
e.camera.autofocus"
android:required="true"/>

<uses-feature
android:name="android.hardwar
e.sensor.accelerometer"
android:required="true"/>
```

```
<uses-feature
android:name="android.hardwar
e.sensor.gyroscope"
android:required="true"/>


<application

android:usesClearTextTraffic=
"true"

    ...>

    <meta-data

android:name="com.google.ar.c
ore"

        android:value="true"
/>

    ...
```

```
</application>
```

3. This will ensure that the app requests the necessary hardware features and permissions to work with ARCore.

Step 3: Create a Basic AR Activity

Now it's time to start adding functionality to your app. We're going to create an activity where you'll render a simple AR object on the screen using ARCore.

1. **Open** `MainActivity.kt`
   Open the **MainActivity.kt** file, which is located under `app/src/main/java/com/you rpackage/`. You'll be replacing its contents with ARCore-related code.

Add   ARCore   Session   Setup

Inside `MainActivity`, start by creating a basic AR session and view setup. Replace the contents of `MainActivity.kt` with

the   following   code:
kotlin

```kotlin
package com.example.ardemo


import android.os.Bundle

import android.widget.Toast

import androidx.appcompat.app.AppCompatActivity

import com.google.ar.core.ArSession

import com.google.ar.core.TrackingState

import com.google.ar.sceneform.ux.ArFragment
```

```kotlin
import
com.google.ar.sceneform.ux.Tr
ansformableNode

import
com.google.ar.sceneform.ux.No
de

import
com.google.ar.sceneform.ux.An
chorNode

import
com.google.ar.sceneform.rende
ring.ModelRenderable


class        MainActivity        :
AppCompatActivity() {


    private    lateinit    var
arFragment: ArFragment
```

```kotlin
    override                fun
onCreate(savedInstanceState:
Bundle?) {

super.onCreate(savedInstanceS
tate)

setContentView(R.layout.activ
ity_main)


        //    Initialize    AR
fragment

        arFragment            =
supportFragmentManager.findFr
agmentById(R.id.ux_fragment)
as ArFragment
```

```
        // Set up the
listener to add the 3D model
when tapped


arFragment.setOnTapArPlaneLis
tener { hitResult, plane,
motionEvent ->

        if (plane.type !=
Plane.Type.HORIZONTAL_UPWARD_
FACING) {


return@setOnTapArPlaneListene
r

        }



        // Create an
anchor at the tapped location
```

```kotlin
val anchor =
hitResult.createAnchor()


// Load the 3D
model and place it at the
anchor point


ModelRenderable.builder()


.setSource(this,
Uri.parse("model.sfb"))    //
replace with the path to your
model

.build()

.thenAccept {
modelRenderable ->
```

```
addNodeToScene(arFragment,
anchor, modelRenderable)

                }


.exceptionally { throwable ->

Toast.makeText(this,      "Error
loading                  model",
Toast.LENGTH_SHORT).show()


return@exceptionally null
                }
        }
    }
```

```kotlin
// Method to add 3D model
to the scene

private                    fun
addNodeToScene(arFragment:
ArFragment,   anchor:   Anchor,
modelRenderable:
ModelRenderable) {

    val    anchorNode   =
AnchorNode(anchor)


anchorNode.setParent(arFragme
nt.arSceneView.scene)


    val    modelNode   =
TransformableNode(arFragment.
transformationSystem)
```

```
modelNode.setParent(anchorNod
e)

        modelNode.renderable
= modelRenderable

    }

}
```

Add AR Fragment to Your Layout
In   the
`res/layout/activity_main.xml`
file, add an `ArFragment` element that will
render the AR content. It should look
something   like   this:
xml

```
<?xml            version="1.0"
encoding="utf-8"?>
```

```xml
<RelativeLayout
xmlns:android="http://schemas
.android.com/apk/res/android"

xmlns:app="http://schemas.and
roid.com/apk/res-auto"

xmlns:tools="http://schemas.a
ndroid.com/tools"

android:layout_width="match_p
arent"

android:layout_height="match_
parent"

android:tools:context=".MainA
ctivity">
```

```xml
<com.google.ar.sceneform.ux.A
rFragment

android:id="@+id/ux_fragment"

android:name="com.google.ar.s
ceneform.ux.ArFragment"

android:layout_width="match_p
arent"

android:layout_height="match_
parent" />

</RelativeLayout>
```

2. **Add a 3D Model for Testing**
   To test your app, you'll need a 3D model. You can either create one or download a simple **.sfb** file. Place the `.sfb` file in the `assets` folder of your project under `src/main/assets/`.

Step 4: Run the App

Now that the code is in place, it's time to run the app on your device to see ARCore in action.

1. **Connect Your Device**
   Ensure that you're using a physical device that supports ARCore. You can verify device compatibility by checking the ARCore supported devices list.
2. **Run the App**
   Press the **Run** button (the green play button) in Android Studio to build and

deploy your app on your connected device.

Step 5: Troubleshooting

If you encounter any issues during setup or testing, here are some tips:

- **ARCore Not Available**:
  If ARCore doesn't appear to work, check if your device is on the supported list. You can also try updating ARCore from the Play Store.
- **Model Not Displaying**:
  Ensure that your model is correctly placed in the `assets` folder, and that you are using the correct path in the `ModelRenderable.builder()` method.

2.4 Understanding Project Structure and File Organization

Now that you have successfully created your first AR project and have a basic understanding of how things are set up, it's time to dive into **project structure and file organization**. Understanding where everything goes in an Android project will help you keep your code neat, organized, and scalable as your app grows.

In this chapter, we'll walk through the basic structure of your **Android AR project**, identify key files and folders, and explain their role. This understanding will help you navigate the project with ease as you work with more complex AR features in the future.

---

1. The Basic Structure of an Android Project

Here's a typical folder structure for an Android project:

css

```
YourProjectName/

├── .git/

├── .gradle/

├── app/

│   ├── build/

│   ├── libs/

│   ├── src/

│   ├── res/

│   ├── AndroidManifest.xml
```

```
|   ├── build.gradle
|   └── proguard-rules.pro
├── gradle/
|   ├── wrapper/
|   └── gradle-wrapper.properties
├── gradle.properties
└── settings.gradle
```

Let's break this down into its core components:

---

2. Key Folders and Files in Your AR Project

1. **app/** – This is the heart of your project, where the actual code, resources, and configurations are stored.

   - **src/**: This folder contains your source code. All your Java and Kotlin files are placed here, organized by package names. The directory typically has two subfolders:

     - **main/**: This is where the majority of your code resides. It contains:

       - **java/**: All Kotlin/Java source files (such as MainActivity

`.kt`) are stored
here.

- **res/**: This is where
  your resources
  such as layouts,
  images, and AR
  models are stored.
  The `res` folder
  contains several
  subfolders:
    - **drawable/**:
      Images and
      graphics,
      such as AR
      models or
      textures.
    - **layout/**:
      XML files
      defining UI
      layouts for
      activities
      and
      fragments.
    - **values/**:
      Stores XML

files for
strings,
colors,
dimensions,
etc.

- **raw/**: Any
  raw files
  like `.sfb`
  models that
  are used by
  ARCore
  (this is
  where we'll
  place 3D
  models in
  your AR
  app).

○ **AndroidManifest.xml**: This
file is essential for defining
your app's metadata and
permissions, like camera access
and ARCore integration, which
we've already added in
previous steps.

- build.gradle: This file contains configuration for the **Gradle build system**, which Android Studio uses to build your app. It defines dependencies, SDK versions, and other essential build configurations.
  - You have two gradle files: one at the project level and another at the app level. The **project-level** `build.gradle` handles global dependencies (like the Android Gradle Plugin), while the **app-level** `build.gradle` contains app-specific dependencies (like ARCore).
- **proguard-rules.pro**: This file is used if you enable ProGuard (or R8) for code obfuscation. For now, we don't need to worry about it unless you want

129

to protect your app's code in
production.

---

3. Main Files and Their Roles

Let's dive deeper into the main components
of your project that are particularly relevant
to AR development:

1. `src/main/java/com/yourpac`
   `kage/MainActivity.kt`
   - This is where you write most of
     your logic. In the first project,
     we defined the ARCore setup
     and view logic here.
   - **MainActivity.kt** is where the
     AR content will be displayed,
     and user interactions (like
     tapping on the screen) will
     trigger certain events (like
     adding 3D objects).
   - You will keep adding code here
     as you build more advanced
     AR features.

2. `src/main/res/layout/activity_main.xml`
    - ○ This XML file is responsible for defining the user interface of your **MainActivity**. Here, we included the `ArFragment` to enable AR rendering.
    - ○ As your app grows, this is where you'll define buttons, menus, or other UI elements.
3. `src/main/res/raw/`
    - ○ The **raw** folder is where you store raw files like **3D models** that ARCore uses. For instance, any `.sfb` (Scene Form Binary) models or `.obj` models should go in this folder.
    - ○ In our project, you could place your AR objects here and load them into the app, as seen in the earlier examples.
4. `AndroidManifest.xml`
    - ○ As you progress with your AR project, you'll need to update

the **AndroidManifest.xml** file with necessary permissions, activities, and services that your app will use.

- o For example, when dealing with AR, you should include permissions to access the camera and the necessary AR features, as seen in earlier chapters.

Here's what the relevant section might look like:
xml

```
<uses-permission
android:name="android.permiss
ion.CAMERA" />

<uses-feature
android:name="android.hardwar
e.camera"
android:required="true"/>
```

```
<uses-feature
android:name="android.hardwar
e.camera.autofocus"
android:required="true"/>
```

---

4. How to Organize Files for Scalability

As your project grows, you may want to organize your files more systematically to keep things manageable. Here's a common way of structuring files in an Android AR project:

1. **Use packages to organize code**:
   - Create a new package under `src/main/java/com/you rpackage/` for different features. For instance:
     - `com.yourpackage.a r`: For AR-related classes (e.g., AR sessions, objects, etc.).

- `com.yourpackage.u` `i`: For UI-related components like activities and fragments.
- `com.yourpackage.u` `tils`: For utility classes or helper methods.

2. **Organize your assets**:
   - If you're working with multiple 3D models, textures, or other large assets, store them in `res/raw/` or `assets/` and use folder structures to organize them.

3. **Version Control with Git**:
   - When your project grows, it's crucial to use version control like **Git**. Ensure to initialize your project with Git early on so that you can track changes, collaborate with others, and roll back to previous versions if needed.

4. **Documentation**:

○ As you add features or make changes, always document your code. This is especially important when working with AR, as it involves many complex systems. Adding comments to explain your logic can help other developers (or yourself) understand the code later on.

---

5. File Organization Best Practices

As you develop your AR app, keep these best practices in mind for better project organization:

- **Separate AR logic from UI code**: Keep your AR code and user interface code in separate classes or even packages to make your app easier to maintain and scale.
- **Keep assets in dedicated folders**: Group models, textures, and other

assets into logically named folders under the `res/raw/` or `assets/` directory.

- **Use Kotlin features for readability**: Kotlin provides excellent features such as extension functions, data classes, and lambdas that can make your code more concise and readable.
- **Leverage Android's ViewModel and LiveData**: These architecture components help in separating the UI and business logic, making your code cleaner and easier to maintain.

2.5 Troubleshooting Setup Issues

Setting up your development environment for Android AR can occasionally present challenges. Whether it's a missing dependency, a misconfigured SDK, or unexpected errors, understanding how to troubleshoot these issues effectively will save you time and frustration. In this chapter, we'll cover common setup problems, their causes, and step-by-step solutions.

---

1. Common Issues During Setup and Their Solutions

Issue 1: Android Studio Fails to Install Correctly

- Problem: The installer fails to complete or Android Studio doesn't launch after installation.
- **Solution**:
  1. Ensure your system meets the minimum requirements for Android Studio. For example:
     - **RAM**: 8 GB minimum (16 GB recommended)
     - **Disk Space**: At least 8 GB
     - **Java Development Kit (JDK)**: Ensure you're using the version

compatible with Android Studio.

2. Re-download the installer from the official Android Studio site to rule out a corrupted file.

3. Run the installer as an administrator on Windows or use sudo for macOS/Linux.

Issue 2: Gradle Sync Errors

- **Problem**: When opening or creating a new project, Gradle fails to sync, showing errors like Could not find com.android.tools.build:gradle.

- **Solution**:
    1. Check your internet connection. Gradle needs to download dependencies during the first sync.
    2. Go to **File > Settings > Gradle** and ensure the following:

- **Gradle JDK**: Use a compatible JDK version (e.g., Java 11 or above).
- **Offline Work**: If enabled, try disabling it to allow dependency downloads.

3. Update the `build.gradle` files:

Ensure your project-level `build.gradle` includes the correct Gradle plugin version: groovy

```
dependencies {

    classpath
'com.android.tools.build:grad
le:8.1.0'

}
```

Clear Gradle cache:
bash

```
rm -rf ~/.gradle/caches/
```

4. Then re-sync the project.

Issue 3: ARCore SDK Not Found

- **Problem**: Errors like `Could not resolve ARCore dependencies`.

- **Solution**:

Verify that ARCore dependencies are added to your `build.gradle` file: groovy

```
implementation
'com.google.ar:core:1.38.0'
```

1. Sync the project again by clicking **File > Sync Project with Gradle Files**.
2. Check your internet connection, as ARCore dependencies are

downloaded from the Maven repository.

If it still fails, manually add the Maven repository:
groovy

```groovy
repositories {

    google()

    mavenCentral()

}
```

Issue 4: Emulator Doesn't Support AR

- **Problem**: AR apps fail to run on the emulator, with errors like `ARCore not supported on this device.`
- **Solution**:
    1. ARCore apps require a compatible physical device for

141

testing. Emulators usually don't support AR.

2. Use a device with ARCore support. Check the ARCore supported devices list.

3. If using an emulator is necessary, enable **camera input** in the emulator settings and use an x86-based system image (with Android 10 or above).

Issue 5: Camera Permission Issues

- **Problem**: The app crashes or shows a blank screen when accessing the AR view.
- **Solution**:

Verify that camera permissions are declared in `AndroidManifest.xml`:
xml

```
<uses-permission
```

```
android:name="android.permiss
ion.CAMERA" />
```

    1.

Add runtime permission handling in your
```
MainActivity:
```
kotlin

```
if
(ContextCompat.checkSelfPermi
ssion(this,
Manifest.permission.CAMERA)

    !=
PackageManager.PERMISSION_GRA
NTED) {


ActivityCompat.requestPermiss
ions(

        this,
```

```
arrayOf(Manifest.permission.C
AMERA),


CAMERA_PERMISSION_REQUEST_COD
E

    )

}
```

Issue 6: Incorrect Device Orientation in AR

- **Problem**: The AR view appears distorted or doesn't align correctly.
- **Solution**:

Ensure your `AndroidManifest.xml` specifies screen orientation: xml

```
<activity
```

```
android:name=".MainActivity"
```

```
android:screenOrientation="la
ndscape" />
```

Use ARCore's APIs to handle orientation changes dynamically: kotlin

```
arFragment.arSceneView.scene.
setOnUpdateListener           {
frameTime ->
```

```
arFragment.onUpdate(frameTime
)
```

```
}
```

2. Debugging Tips

Check Logs with Logcat

- Use Android Studio's **Logcat** tool to view detailed error messages.
- Apply filters to focus on your app's logs:
  - **Filter by package name**: This shows logs specific to your app.
  - **Set log levels**: Use $Error$ or $Debug$ to identify issues.

Example:
bash

```
E/ARCore:        Failed        to
initialize session
```

Validate Dependencies

- Verify that all required libraries are installed. Open **SDK Manager** in Android Studio and ensure:
  - **Android SDK Build-Tools**
  - **Google Play Services for AR**

146

- **Google Repository**

Check Device Compatibility

- Ensure your physical device supports ARCore:
  - Test using the **ARCore App from Play Store**.

Enable Developer Options

- On your Android device, enable **Developer Options** and **USB Debugging** to allow seamless testing and debugging.

---

3. Preventive Measures

1. **Keep Everything Updated**:
   - Regularly update Android Studio, ARCore, and your project dependencies to avoid compatibility issues.
2. **Backup Projects**:

- Use Git or another version control system to back up your projects regularly.

3. **Document Issues and Solutions**:
   - Maintain a personal troubleshooting log for quick reference in future projects.

---

4. Example Scenario: Fixing a Gradle Dependency Error

Here's a practical example of resolving a missing ARCore dependency:

Error Message:

```
Could        not        resolve
com.google.ar:core:1.38.0
```

Solution:

Add the correct repository in your `build.gradle` file: groovy

```groovy
repositories {

    google()

    mavenCentral()

}
```

1. Check if your internet connection is active and Gradle is not in offline mode.
2. Force sync Gradle:
   - In Android Studio, click **File > Sync Project with Gradle Files**.

Result: After the sync completes, the ARCore library will be successfully included in your project.

Hands-On Project: Set Up and Run Your First Kotlin-Based Android AR App

This project will guide you through the process of setting up, creating, and running your first Kotlin-based Android AR app using ARCore. By the end of this chapter, you'll have a working app that displays basic AR functionality and prepares you for more complex projects.

---

1. Objectives

- Set up a basic Kotlin Android AR project.
- Understand how ARCore initializes and interacts with your app.
- Build and run a functional AR app.

---

2. Prerequisites

Before proceeding, ensure the following:

1. **Android Studio**: Installed and configured with Kotlin support.
2. **ARCore and SDKs**: Set up as outlined in earlier chapters.
3. **A Supported Android Device**: Ensure it's ARCore-compatible.
4. **USB Debugging Enabled**: For device testing.

---

3. Steps to Create Your First AR App

Step 1: Create a New Android Project

1. Open Android Studio.
2. Click on **File > New Project**.
3. Choose **Empty Activity** as your template and click **Next**.
4. Configure your project:
   - **Name**: FirstKotlinARApp
   - **Package Name**: com.example.firstkotlinar
   - **Language**: Kotlin

- ○ **Minimum API Level**: Select
  API 24 (Android 7.0) or higher.
5. Click **Finish** to generate the project.

Step 2: Configure Your Project for ARCore

Open your project's `build.gradle` file (app-level) and add ARCore as a dependency:
groovy

```
dependencies {

    implementation
'com.google.ar:core:1.38.0'

}
```

1. Sync the project by clicking **File > Sync Project with Gradle Files**.

Step 3: Update the Manifest File

Add ARCore permissions and requirements to the `AndroidManifest.xml` file:

xml

```
<uses-permission
android:name="android.permiss
ion.CAMERA" />

<uses-feature
android:name="android.hardwar
e.camera.ar"
android:required="true" />
```

Step 4: Add AR Fragment to Your Layout

1. Open the res/layout/activity_main. xml file.

Replace the existing ConstraintLayout with the Fragment for AR: xml

```
<?xml version="1.0"
encoding="utf-8"?>

<fragment


xmlns:android="http://schemas
.android.com/apk/res/android"


android:id="@+id/arFragment"
```

```
android:name="com.google.ar.s
ceneform.ux.ArFragment"
```

```
android:layout_width="match_p
arent"
```

```
android:layout_height="match_
parent" />
```

2.

Step 5: Write the MainActivity Code

1. Open `MainActivity.kt`.
2. Replace the existing code with the following:

kotlin

```
package
com.example.firstkotlinar


import android.os.Bundle

import
com.google.ar.sceneform.ux.Ar
Fragment

import
androidx.appcompat.app.AppCom
patActivity

import
com.google.ar.core.Anchor

import
com.google.ar.sceneform.Ancho
rNode

import
com.google.ar.sceneform.rende
ring.ModelRenderable
```

```kotlin
import
com.google.ar.sceneform.ux.Tr
ansformableNode


class       MainActivity       :
AppCompatActivity() {


    private     lateinit     var
arFragment: ArFragment


    override                  fun
onCreate(savedInstanceState:
Bundle?) {


super.onCreate(savedInstanceS
tate)
```

```kotlin
setContentView(R.layout.activ
ity_main)


        // Initialize AR
Fragment
        arFragment           =
supportFragmentManager.findFr
agmentById(R.id.arFragment)
as ArFragment


        // Set up a tap
listener to place objects in
AR

arFragment.setOnTapArPlaneLis
tener { hitResult, _, _ ->
```

```kotlin
placeObject(hitResult.createA
nchor())

        }

    }


    private                    fun
placeObject(anchor: Anchor) {

ModelRenderable.builder()

            .setSource(this,
R.raw.android_robot)  //  Load
a 3D model from res/raw

            .build()

            .thenAccept        {
modelRenderable ->
```

```kotlin
val anchorNode = AnchorNode(anchor).apply {

    setParent(arFragment.arSceneView.scene)

}


val transformableNode = TransformableNode(arFragment.transformationSystem).apply {

    setParent(anchorNode)

    renderable = modelRenderable

    select()
```

```
                    }

               }

          .exceptionally    {
throwable ->


throwable.printStackTrace()

               null

          }

     }

}
```

---

4. Add a 3D Model

1. Download a `.glb` or `.gltf` 3D
   model (e.g., an Android robot).
2. Place it in the `res/raw` directory:

161

- o **File Name**: android_robot.glb.
- o Create the raw folder if it doesn't exist.

5. Run Your App

1. Connect your ARCore-compatible Android device.
2. Click **Run > Run App** or press **Shift+F10**.
3. Allow camera permissions when prompted.
4. Tap on a flat surface in your environment to place the 3D model.

6. Expected Output

- The app will launch and display a live camera feed.
- Tap on any flat surface detected by ARCore.

162

- A 3D Android robot model will appear on the tapped surface and can be rotated or resized using gestures.

---

7. Detailed Code Explanation

AR Fragment

- The `ArFragment` class handles most ARCore setup:
    - Detects planes.
    - Manages camera input.
    - Provides transformation tools.

Tap Listener

kotlin

```
arFragment.setOnTapArPlaneLis
tener { hitResult, _, _ ->


placeObject(hitResult.createA
nchor())
```

```
}
```

- Responds to user taps on detected planes.
- Creates an Anchor at the tapped position.

3D Model Loading

kotlin

```
ModelRenderable.builder()

    .setSource(this,
R.raw.android_robot)

    .build()

    .thenAcccpt                    {
modelRenderable -> ... }
```

- Asynchronously loads the 3D model and applies it to the scene.

Anchor and Transformable Nodes

- **AnchorNode**: Represents a fixed position in the AR scene.
- **TransformableNode**: Adds gestures (move, rotate, scale) to 3D models.

---

8. Troubleshooting

1. **Error: Model File Not Found**:
   - Ensure the `.glb` file is in the `res/raw` directory.
   - Verify the file name matches `R.raw.android_robot`.
2. **ARCore Compatibility Issue**:
   - Test on an ARCore-supported device.

- Ensure Google Play Services for AR is installed on the device.
3. **Object Not Appearing**:
    - Check if the app detects planes by looking for the plane grid overlay.
    - Ensure sufficient lighting in the testing environment.

---

9. Next Steps

Now that you've successfully set up and run your first Kotlin-based AR app, the next chapters will guide you in adding interactivity, animations, and advanced AR features to enhance your app. Keep experimenting with different 3D models and layouts to deepen your understanding of AR development!

Conclusion

With this chapter, your development environment is now ready, and you've created your first AR app using Kotlin. This foundation sets the stage for more advanced projects and features, which we'll dive into in the following chapters. Let's continue building!

Chapter 3: Kotlin Basics for AR Development

Kotlin is a modern programming language that combines simplicity, readability, and power, making it a perfect choice for AR development. In this chapter, we'll explore the foundational Kotlin concepts that you'll use throughout this book to build AR applications.

3.1 Variables, Data Types, and Functions in Kotlin

Kotlin, as a language, shines in its simplicity and expressiveness. Mastering its basics, like variables, data types, and functions, is essential for building dynamic AR applications. This chapter provides a deep dive into these foundational concepts, ensuring you're equipped to write clean and efficient code.

168

Variables in Kotlin

Immutable Variables (`val`)

Kotlin encourages immutability. Variables declared with `val` cannot be reassigned after their initial value is set. This ensures stability and reduces bugs.

Example:

kotlin

```
val appName = "AR Explorer"
// Immutable variable

println(appName)


// Uncommenting the next line
would cause an error
```

```
//    appName   =   "New   AR
Explorer"
```

Mutable Variables (`var`)

When a variable needs to be reassigned, use
`var`. This is common in scenarios like
counters or mutable states.

Example:

kotlin

```
var userScore = 0  // Mutable
variable

println("Initial        Score:
$userScore")


userScore += 10  // Reassign
value
```

```
println("Updated        Score:
$userScore")
```

Data Types in Kotlin

Kotlin is a statically-typed language, meaning each variable has a defined type. Kotlin can infer types automatically, but you can also declare them explicitly for clarity.

Common Data Types

- **Numeric**: Byte, Short, Int, Long, Float, Double
- **Text**: String, Char
- **Logical**: Boolean
- **Collections**: Array, List, Set, Map

Explicit Declaration:

kotlin

```
val userAge: Int = 25

val pi: Double = 3.14159

val isArEnabled: Boolean =
true
```

Type Inference:

kotlin

```
val userName = "Alex"    //
Inferred as String

val maxSpeed = 120       //
Inferred as Int
```

Strings in Kotlin

Strings in Kotlin are highly versatile and allow embedding variables using string templates.

Example:

kotlin

```
val firstName = "John"

val lastName = "Doe"

val fullName = "$firstName $lastName"   // String template

println("Welcome, $fullName!")
```

Functions in Kotlin

Functions are the backbone of Kotlin applications, enabling reusable blocks of code.

Basic Syntax

A function is declared using the `fun` keyword.

Example:

kotlin

```
fun greetUser(name: String): String {
    return "Hello, $name! Welcome to Kotlin AR."
```

```
}
```

Calling a Function:

kotlin

```
val        message        =
greetUser("Alice")

println(message)
```

Default and Named Parameters

Kotlin allows you to define default values for function parameters, making your code cleaner and more flexible.

Example:

kotlin

```kotlin
fun     calculateScore(points:
Int = 10, bonus: Int = 5):
Int {

    return points + bonus

}
```

```kotlin
val         totalScore      =
calculateScore(bonus    =    15)
// Named parameter

println("Total         Score:
$totalScore")
```

Unit Functions

If a function doesn't return a value, it's of
type Unit.

Example:

kotlin

```kotlin
fun printWelcomeMessage() {

    println("Welcome          to
Kotlin AR Development!")

}
```

Hands-On Example: Variables, Data Types, and Functions

Let's create a small program to manage AR objects in a virtual scene.

Step 1: Define Variables

Define some variables to represent an AR object's name, position, and state.

kotlin

```kotlin
val objectName = "Virtual Cube"

var position = "Table"

var isVisible = true
```

Step 2: Write a Function to Display Object Details

kotlin

```kotlin
fun displayObjectDetails(name: String, position: String, visible: Boolean): String {

    val visibility = if (visible) "visible" else "hidden"
```

```kotlin
    return    "$name    is
$visibility    at    position:
$position"

}
```

Step 3: Call the Function and Print the Output

kotlin

```kotlin
fun main() {

    val    objectDetails    =
displayObjectDetails(objectNa
me, position, isVisible)

    println(objectDetails)


    // Update position and
visibility
```

179

```
    position = "Floor"

    isVisible = false



println(displayObjectDetails(
objectName,          position,
isVisible))

}
```

Output:

mathematica

```
Virtual  Cube  is  visible  at
position: Table

Virtual  Cube  is  hidden  at
position: Floor
```

Key Takeaways

1. **Variables**: Use `val` for constants and `var` for mutable data.
2. **Data Types**: Understand how Kotlin handles numbers, text, and collections.
3. **Functions**: Master basic function syntax and leverage default/named parameters for flexibility.
4. **String Templates**: Simplify your code with embedded variables.

By combining these basic building blocks, you've laid a strong foundation for coding in Kotlin. In the next section, we'll explore control flow structures like loops and conditionals to enhance your programs further!

3.2 Control Flow: Loops and Conditionals

Control flow structures are essential in programming, as they allow your application to make decisions and repeat tasks efficiently. In Kotlin, control flow is managed through conditionals like "`if`" statements and loops such as "`for`" and "`while`". This chapter will walk you through these constructs with practical examples to ensure you grasp how they can be applied in AR development.

Conditionals in Kotlin

The `if` Statement

The `if` statement allows your program to execute a block of code only if a specified condition is true.

Example:

kotlin

```
val isARSupported = true

if (isARSupported) {

    println("AR is supported
on this device!")

} else {

    println("AR    is    not
supported on this device.")

}
```

Using `if` as an Expression:

Kotlin allows `if` to return a value, making it versatile for variable assignment.

kotlin

```
val deviceStatus = if
(isARSupported) "Supported"
else "Not Supported"

println("Device Status:
$deviceStatus")
```

The `when` Statement

The `when` statement is Kotlin's enhanced version of the traditional `switch` statement. It's clean, concise, and supports multiple conditions.

Example:

kotlin

```kotlin
val arMode = "Surface Detection"

val description = when (arMode) {
    "Surface Detection" -> "Detecting flat surfaces for object placement."
    "Face Tracking" -> "Tracking faces for AR overlays."
    else -> "Unknown AR mode."
}
```

```
println(description)
```

Loops in Kotlin

The `for` Loop

A `for` loop is ideal for iterating over ranges, collections, or arrays.

Iterating Over a Range:

kotlin

```
for (i in 1..5) {
    println("Loop    iteration:
$i")

}
```

Iterating Over an Array:

kotlin

```kotlin
val arObjects =
arrayOf("Cube", "Sphere",
"Pyramid")


for (obj in arObjects) {
    println("Rendering     AR
Object: $obj")
}
```

The while Loop

The `while` loop repeats a block of code as long as a condition is true.

Example:

kotlin

```kotlin
var batteryLevel = 100

while (batteryLevel > 0) {
    println("Battery at $batteryLevel%. Continuing AR session...")

    batteryLevel -= 20
}
```

```
println("Battery      depleted.
Exiting AR session.")
```

The do-while Loop

This loop is similar to while, but it guarantees the block runs at least once.

Example:

kotlin

```
var isSessionActive = false

do {
    println("Attempting      to
start AR session...")

    isSessionActive = true
```

```kotlin
} while (!isSessionActive)


println("AR   session   started
successfully!")
```

Combining Loops and Conditionals

In AR development, loops and conditionals often work together. For instance, you might need to render multiple AR objects based on a condition.

Example: Render Only Visible AR Objects

kotlin

```kotlin
data class ARObject(val name:
String,     val     isVisible:
Boolean)


val objects = listOf(

    ARObject("Cube", true),

    ARObject("Sphere",
false),

    ARObject("Pyramid", true)

)


for (obj in objects) {

    if (obj.isVisible) {

        println("Rendering  AR
Object: ${obj.name}")
```

```
        }

}
```

Output:

javascript

```
Rendering AR Object: Cube

Rendering AR Object: Pyramid
```

Hands-On Example: AR Object Placement with Loops and Conditionals

Let's create a Kotlin console program to manage and place AR objects in a virtual scene.

Step 1: Define AR Object Data

Create a data class to represent AR objects.

kotlin

```
data class ARObject(val name:
String, var position: String,
var isPlaced: Boolean)
```

Step 2: Create a List of Objects

kotlin

```
val        arObjects      =
mutableListOf(
```

```
    ARObject("Cube",      "Not
Placed", false),

    ARObject("Sphere",    "Not
Placed", false),

    ARObject("Pyramid",   "Not
Placed", false)

)
```

Step 3: Write a Function to Place Objects

kotlin

```
fun            placeObject(obj:
ARObject, position: String) {

    obj.position = position

    obj.isPlaced = true
```

```
    println("${obj.name}
placed at $position.")
}
```

Step 4: Loop Through and Place Objects

kotlin

```
for (obj in arObjects) {
    if (!obj.isPlaced) {
        placeObject(obj,
"Table")
    }
}
```

Full Code Example

kotlin

```kotlin
data class ARObject(val name:
String, var position: String,
var isPlaced: Boolean)


fun          placeObject(obj:
ARObject, position: String) {
    obj.position = position

    obj.isPlaced = true

    println("${obj.name}
placed at $position.")
}


fun main() {
```

```
val      arObjects      =
mutableListOf(

    ARObject("Cube",  "Not
Placed", false),

    ARObject("Sphere",
"Not Placed", false),

    ARObject("Pyramid",
"Not Placed", false)

)


for (obj in arObjects) {

    if (!obj.isPlaced) {

        placeObject(obj,
"Table")

    }

}
```

```
}
```

Output:

mathematica

```
Cube placed at Table.

Sphere placed at Table.

Pyramid placed at Table.
```

Key Takeaways

1. **Conditionals**: Use `if` for simple decisions and `when` for complex multi-branch logic.

2. **Loops**: Utilize `for`, `while`, and `do-while` loops based on your iteration needs.
3. **Combination**: Combine loops and conditionals to handle dynamic data effectively.
4. **Real-World Application**: Start thinking about how these concepts can automate repetitive tasks in AR development, like object placement.

In the next section, we'll explore Kotlin's object-oriented programming features, which are crucial for structuring AR applications.

3.3 Kotlin Classes and Objects: OOP Principles

Object-Oriented Programming (OOP) is a foundational paradigm in software development, and Kotlin fully embraces it.

199

By using classes and objects, you can model real-world scenarios in your code, making it easier to design, maintain, and scale applications. This chapter will explore Kotlin's OOP principles and provide practical examples to ensure you master them for AR development.

Why OOP Matters in AR Development

Augmented Reality apps often involve complex entities, such as virtual objects, scenes, and user interactions. Using OOP allows you to structure these entities into reusable and manageable components.

For example:

- A **class** can represent an AR object (e.g., a cube or a sphere).
- **Objects** are instances of those classes with specific attributes (e.g., color, size, position).

- **Methods** allow the objects to perform actions (e.g., move or rotate).

Defining a Class in Kotlin

A class is a blueprint for creating objects. It defines the properties (data) and methods (functions) of the objects.

Basic Class Example

kotlin

```
class ARObject(val name:
String, var position: String)
{

    fun moveTo(newPosition:
String) {

        position =
newPosition
```

```kotlin
        println("$name    moved
to $newPosition.")

    }

}
```

Here's what's happening:

- `val name`: A read-only property, as the object's name shouldn't change.
- `var position`: A mutable property representing the object's position.
- `moveTo()`: A method to update the object's position.

Creating an Object

You can create an instance of a class using the `constructor`.

kotlin

```kotlin
val cube = ARObject("Cube",
"Table")

cube.moveTo("Floor")
```

Output:

mathematica

```
Cube moved to Floor.
```

Primary and Secondary Constructors

Kotlin simplifies class creation with **primary constructors**.

Example with Primary Constructor

kotlin

```kotlin
class ARObject(val name:
String, var position: String)
```

For additional initialization, you can use **secondary constructors**.

Example with Secondary Constructor

kotlin

```kotlin
class ARObject(val name:
String, var position: String)
{

    constructor(name: String)
: this(name, "Unknown")

}
```

This allows you to create an object with only a name:

kotlin

```kotlin
val sphere = ARObject("Sphere")

println("${sphere.name} is at ${sphere.position}.")
```

Output:

csharp

```
Sphere is at Unknown.
```

Encapsulation: Keeping Data Safe

Encapsulation hides the internal details of an object, exposing only what's necessary. This is achieved using access modifiers like private, protected, and public (default).

Example of Encapsulation

kotlin

```kotlin
class ARObject(private val
name: String, private var
position: String) {

    fun getName() = name

    fun getPosition() =
position

    fun moveTo(newPosition:
String) {
```

```kotlin
        position              =
newPosition

        println("$name    moved
to $position.")

    }

}
```

Now, you can only interact with the object through its methods:

kotlin

```kotlin
val          pyramid          =
ARObject("Pyramid", "Desk")

println("${pyramid.getName()}
is                         at
${pyramid.getPosition()}.")

pyramid.moveTo("Shelf")
```

Inheritance: Reusing Code

Inheritance allows you to create a new class based on an existing one, reusing its properties and methods.

Base and Derived Class Example

kotlin

```kotlin
open class ARObject(val name:
String, var position: String)
{

    fun    moveTo(newPosition:
String) {

        position          =
newPosition
```

```kotlin
        println("$name   moved
to $position.")

    }

}


class
InteractiveARObject(name:
String, position: String, val
interaction:    String)    :
ARObject(name, position) {

    fun interact() {

        println("$name    is
$interaction.")

    }

}
```

Usage

kotlin

```kotlin
val interactiveCube = InteractiveARObject("Interactive Cube", "Desk", "rotating")

interactiveCube.moveTo("Table")

interactiveCube.interact()
```

Output:

mathematica

```
Interactive Cube moved to Table.
```

```
Interactive Cube is rotating.
```

Polymorphism: Extending Behavior

Polymorphism allows objects to take many forms, enabling you to use the same interface for different underlying implementations.

Example: Overriding a Method

kotlin

```
open class ARObject(val name:
String, var position: String)
{

    open fun describe() {

        println("$name        is
located at $position.")
```

```kotlin
        }

    }


    class    DynamicARObject(name:
    String,   position:   String)   :
    ARObject(name, position) {

        override fun describe() {

            println("$name         is
    dynamically      placed      at
    $position.")

        }

    }
```

Usage

kotlin

```
val  cube  =  ARObject("Cube",
"Floor")

val     dynamicSphere     =
DynamicARObject("Sphere",
"Table")


cube.describe()

dynamicSphere.describe()
```

Output:

mathematica

```
Cube is located at Floor.

Sphere is dynamically placed
at Table.
```

Hands-On Example: Modeling AR Objects with OOP

Let's build a simple program to simulate AR object management using OOP principles.

Step 1: Define the Base Class

kotlin

```
open class ARObject(val name:
String, var position: String)
{

    open                    fun
place(newPosition: String) {

        position            =
newPosition
```

```kotlin
        println("$name placed
at $position.")
    }

}
```

Step 2: Add a Specialized Class

kotlin

```kotlin
class    MovableARObject(name:
String, position: String, var
isMovable:      Boolean)      :
ARObject(name, position) {

    fun      move(newPosition:
String) {

        if (isMovable) {
```

```kotlin
        place(newPosition)

        } else {

            println("$name
cannot be moved.")

        }

    }

}
```

Step 3: Implement the Program

kotlin

```kotlin
fun main() {

    val         cube        =
MovableARObject("Cube",
"Desk", true)
```

216

```
    val       statue       =
MovableARObject("Statue",
"Floor", false)


    cube.move("Table")

    statue.move("Shelf")
}
```

Output:

mathematica

```
Cube placed at Table.

Statue cannot be moved.
```

Key Takeaways

- **Classes and Objects**: Use classes to define AR entities and objects to represent them.
- **Encapsulation**: Protect object data and expose only necessary methods.
- **Inheritance**: Extend base classes for reusable code.
- **Polymorphism**: Enable flexible behavior for different object types.

Understanding and applying these OOP principles will enable you to design robust AR applications. Next, we'll explore Kotlin Coroutines for handling asynchronous tasks, a crucial skill for AR development.

3.4 Understanding Kotlin Coroutines and Asynchronous Programming

Kotlin Coroutines are a powerful and elegant way to manage asynchronous programming in Android development. They help you write clean, readable, and efficient code without the complexity of traditional callback mechanisms or thread management.

In this chapter, we will explore:

1. The fundamentals of coroutines.
2. Key coroutine concepts and APIs.
3. Practical examples of using coroutines in Android applications.

Why Coroutines?

Asynchronous programming is essential when dealing with tasks like:

- Fetching data from a network.
- Performing database operations.

- Managing long-running computations.

Traditional approaches, such as threads or callbacks, often lead to:

- Callback hell (nested callbacks that are hard to read and debug).
- Complex thread management.
- Increased potential for errors like memory leaks.

Coroutines simplify this by providing a structured and efficient way to handle asynchronous tasks.

What are Coroutines?

A coroutine is a lightweight thread-like structure that allows you to execute asynchronous code sequentially. Instead of blocking a thread, coroutines suspend execution at specific points and resume later.

Key Benefits

- **Lightweight:** Coroutines are much lighter than threads, allowing you to run thousands of them without performance issues.
- **Readable Code:** They enable sequential, synchronous-like code for asynchronous operations.
- **Built-in Error Handling:** Coroutines have structured concurrency that helps manage errors effectively.

Setting Up Coroutines in Your Project

Before using coroutines, ensure the required dependency is added to your project.

Add Coroutine Dependency

In your `build.gradle` file:

groovy

```
implementation
"org.jetbrains.kotlinx:kotlin
x-coroutines-core:1.7.3"

implementation
"org.jetbrains.kotlinx:kotlin
x-coroutines-android:1.7.3"
```

Sync your project after adding the dependencies.

Understanding Coroutine Basics

Coroutine Scope

A coroutine scope defines the lifecycle of coroutines. Common scopes include:

- `GlobalScope`: Lifetime of the application,

- **CoroutineScope**: Custom-defined scope.
- **ViewModelScope**: Scoped to the lifecycle of a ViewModel.

Launching a Coroutine

You can launch a coroutine using the launch or async builders within a scope.

Example: Basic Coroutine

kotlin

```
import kotlinx.coroutines.*


fun main() = runBlocking {

    println("Start:
${Thread.currentThread().name
}")
```

```kotlin
launch {

    delay(1000L)          //
Suspend the coroutine for 1
second

    println("Inside
coroutine:
${Thread.currentThread().name
}")

    }



    println("End:
${Thread.currentThread().name
}")

}
```

Output:

yaml

```
Start: main

End: main

Inside coroutine: main
```

Suspending Functions

Suspending functions pause execution without blocking threads. Use the suspend modifier to define them.

Example

kotlin

```kotlin
suspend fun fetchUserData():
String {

    delay(2000L)  // Simulate
network delay

    return "User Data Loaded"
}


fun main() = runBlocking {

    val        data        =
fetchUserData()

    println(data)

}
```

Coroutines in Android Development

In Android, coroutines help prevent freezing the UI thread during long-running operations.

Example: Updating the UI with Coroutine

kotlin

```
import android.os.Bundle

import
androidx.appcompat.app.AppCom
patActivity

import kotlinx.coroutines.*


class        MainActivity     :
AppCompatActivity() {
```

```kotlin
    override              fun
onCreate(savedInstanceState:
Bundle?) {

super.onCreate(savedInstanceS
tate)

setContentView(R.layout.activ
ity_main)


    // Use  the  MainScope
for UI-related coroutines
    val     uiScope    =
MainScope()


    uiScope.launch {
```

```kotlin
        val    data    =
fetchUserData()

        updateUI(data)

    }

}


    private    suspend    fun
fetchUserData(): String {

        delay(2000L)        //
Simulate network delay

        return    "Hello,    AR
World!"

    }


    private            fun
updateUI(data: String) {
```

```kotlin
        println(data)        //
Replace with actual UI update
code

    }


    override fun onDestroy()
{

        super.onDestroy()

        uiScope.cancel()    //
Cancel the scope to avoid
memory leaks

    }

}
```

Using async for Concurrent Tasks

The async builder runs tasks concurrently and returns a Deferred result, which you can await.

Example: Fetch Data Concurrently

kotlin

```
suspend                      fun
fetchDataFromServer():  String
{

    delay(1000L)

    return "Server Data"

}
```

```kotlin
suspend                    fun
fetchDataFromDatabase():
String {

    delay(1500L)

    return "Database Data"

}


fun main() = runBlocking {

    val serverData = async {
fetchDataFromServer() }

    val databaseData = async
{ fetchDataFromDatabase() }


    println("Combined Result:
${serverData.await()}         +
${databaseData.await()}")
```

```
}
```

Output:

arduino

```
Combined  Result:  Server  Data
+ Database Data
```

Handling Errors in Coroutines

Errors in coroutines can be managed using
structured concurrency and exception
handlers.

Example: Coroutine Exception Handling

kotlin

```kotlin
fun main() = runBlocking {

    val handler =
CoroutineExceptionHandler {
_, exception ->

        println("Caught
exception:
${exception.message}")

    }


    val scope =
CoroutineScope(SupervisorJob(
) + handler)


    scope.launch {

        throw
RuntimeException("Something
went wrong!")
```

```
    }


    delay(1000L)    // Wait for
coroutine to complete

}
```

Hands-On Example: Async Data Fetch for AR

Let's create a basic program to simulate fetching AR object data from multiple sources.

Step 1: Define Suspended Functions

kotlin

```kotlin
suspend fun fetchARModel():
String {

    delay(1000L)  // Simulate
network delay

    return "AR Model Data"

}


suspend fun fetchARTexture():
String {

    delay(1500L)  // Simulate
network delay

    return "AR Texture Data"

}
```

Step 2: Use Coroutines for Concurrent Fetching

kotlin

```kotlin
fun main() = runBlocking {

    println("Fetching        AR
Data...")


    val   model  =  async  {
fetchARModel() }
    val  texture  =  async  {
fetchARTexture() }


    println("Model:
${model.await()}")
    println("Texture:
${texture.await()}")
```

```
}
```

Key Takeaways

1. **Coroutine Builders**: Use `launch` for fire-and-forget tasks, `async` for concurrent tasks with results.
2. **Suspending Functions**: Simplify asynchronous tasks with sequential code.
3. **Error Handling**: Use `CoroutineExceptionHandler` for robust error management.

Mastering Kotlin Coroutines is essential for building AR apps that require smooth and responsive experiences. Up next, we'll explore Kotlin Extensions to simplify AR code and streamline your development workflow.

3.5 Using Kotlin Extensions for Simplifying AR Code

Kotlin extensions are a remarkable feature that allows developers to add functionality to existing classes without modifying their source code. This feature can significantly simplify your AR development workflow by enabling cleaner, more modular, and reusable code.

In this chapter, we will explore:

1. What Kotlin extensions are.
2. How to create and use extension functions and properties.
3. Practical examples to simplify AR-related code.

What Are Kotlin Extensions?

Kotlin extensions allow you to extend a class's functionality by adding new methods or properties to it. These extensions do not modify the actual class but provide a syntactic sugar that feels like the functionality is part of the class.

For example, you can extend a `Vector3` class (used in ARCore for 3D coordinates) to add a method that calculates the distance between two points.

Advantages of Kotlin Extensions

- **Improved Readability:** Encapsulate repetitive logic into extensions for cleaner code.
- **Reusable Code:** Write methods once and use them across multiple parts of your project.
- **Modular Design:** Keep the original classes untouched, adhering to the principle of separation of concerns.

Creating Kotlin Extension Functions

An extension function is a function added to a class. You define it by specifying the class name as a receiver type followed by the function name.

Syntax

kotlin

```
fun
ClassName.functionName(parame
ters): ReturnType {

    // Function body

}
```

Example: Adding a Function to a Class

Let's add a function to Float to convert degrees to radians, useful in AR for rotation calculations.

kotlin

```kotlin
fun Float.toRadians(): Float
=
Math.toRadians(this.toDouble(
)).toFloat()


// Usage

val degrees = 90f

val        radians         =
degrees.toRadians()

println("Radians:   $radians")
// Output: Radians: 1.5707964
```

Using Extensions in AR Development

Extensions can simplify AR-related code by encapsulating common operations.

Example 1: Calculating Distance Between Two Points

In ARCore, the `Vector3` class is commonly used for 3D coordinates. Let's create an extension function to calculate the distance between two points.

kotlin

```
import
com.google.ar.sceneform.math.
Vector3

import kotlin.math.sqrt
```

```kotlin
fun Vector3.distanceTo(other:
Vector3): Float {

    return sqrt(

        (this.x - other.x) *
(this.x - other.x) +

        (this.y - other.y) *
(this.y - other.y) +

        (this.z - other.z) *
(this.z - other.z)

    )

}


// Usage

val point1 = Vector3(1f, 2f,
3f)
```

```kotlin
val point2 = Vector3(4f, 5f,
6f)


val            distance        =
point1.distanceTo(point2)

println("Distance:
$distance")         //    Output:
Distance: 5.196152
```

Example 2: Simplifying Anchor Creation

Anchors are crucial in ARCore for placing objects in the real world. Here's an extension function to simplify creating an anchor at a specific position.

kotlin

```kotlin
import
com.google.ar.core.Anchor

import
com.google.ar.sceneform.Ancho
rNode

import
com.google.ar.sceneform.Scene


fun
Scene.createAnchorAt(position
: Vector3): AnchorNode {

    val          anchor          =
this.arFrame!!.hitTest(positi
on.x,
position.y).firstOrNull()?.cr
eateAnchor()

    return
AnchorNode(anchor).apply      {
```

```kotlin
        this.setParent(this@createAnc
horAt) }

    }


// Usage

val       scene:      Scene    =
arFragment.arSceneView.scene

val   position   =   Vector3(0f,
0f, -1f)


val          anchorNode        =
scene.createAnchorAt(position
)

println("Anchor   created   at:
$position")
```

Example 3: Updating Node Transformations

Let's create an extension function for `TransformableNode` to easily update its position.

kotlin

```
import
com.google.ar.sceneform.ux.Tr
ansformableNode


fun
TransformableNode.updatePosit
ion(newPosition: Vector3) {

    this.worldPosition        =
newPosition
```

```kotlin
}


// Usage

val node =
TransformableNode(arFragment.
transformationSystem)

val newPosition = Vector3(1f,
1f, 1f)


node.updatePosition(newPositi
on)

println("Node updated to:
$newPosition")
```

Creating Extension Properties

Extension properties work like regular properties but are defined outside the class. They're useful for adding calculated properties to classes.

Example: Midpoint Between Two Vectors

Add a property to calculate the midpoint between two Vector3 points.

kotlin

```
val              Pair<Vector3,
Vector3>.midpoint: Vector3

    get() = Vector3(

        (first.x  +  second.x)
 / 2,
```

```kotlin
        (first.y  +  second.y)
/ 2,

        (first.z  +  second.z)
/ 2

    )



// Usage

val  point1  =  Vector3(1f,  1f,
1f)

val  point2  =  Vector3(3f,  3f,
3f)



val  midpoint  =  (point1  to
point2).midpoint

println("Midpoint:
$midpoint")       //    Output:
Midpoint: (2.0, 2.0, 2.0)
```

Practical Tips for Using Extensions

1. **Keep It Contextual**: Create extensions only for logic frequently reused in the same context.
2. **Avoid Overuse**: Overloading classes with extensions can make code less intuitive.
3. **Document Extensions**: Clearly document what your extension does and where it should be used.

Hands-On Example: Simplifying AR Object Placement

Let's create a small utility using extensions to simplify placing objects in AR.

Step 1: Define the Extension

We'll add a utility function to place an AR object at a specific world position.

kotlin

```
import
com.google.ar.sceneform.ux.Tr
ansformableNode

import
com.google.ar.sceneform.math.
Vector3

import
com.google.ar.sceneform.Scene


fun
Scene.placeObjectAt(position:
Vector3, modelResource: Int):
TransformableNode {
```

```kotlin
    val       anchor      =
this.createAnchorAt(position)

    return
TransformableNode(arFragment.
transformationSystem).apply {

        setParent(anchor)

        renderable        =
ModelRenderable.builder()


.setSource(context,
modelResource)

            .build()

            .get()

        select()

    }

}
```

Step 2: Use the Extension

kotlin

```
val position = Vector3(0f,
0f, -1f)

scene.placeObjectAt(position,
R.raw.my_3d_model)
```

Hands-On Project: Build a Kotlin-Based Console App to Simulate AR Object Placement Logic

In this project, we'll create a Kotlin-based console application to simulate object placement in a 3D space, similar to what AR

255

apps do. This exercise will give you foundational knowledge of AR concepts, including 3D coordinates, transformations, and object interactions, in a simple, controlled environment.

Project Overview

We will:

1. Create a Kotlin console app.
2. Define a 3D space with x, y, z coordinates.
3. Simulate object placement and movement.
4. Visualize object information in a readable format.

Step 1: Setting Up the Kotlin Console App

To start, let's sct up a simple Kotlin project.

1.1 Creating a Kotlin Project in IntelliJ IDEA

1. Open IntelliJ IDEA.
2. Select **File > New > Project**.
3. Choose **Kotlin** and select **JVM**.
4. Name your project (e.g., *ARObjectSimulator*) and set the destination folder.
5. Click **Finish** to create the project.

1.2 Setting Up the `main.kt` File

Create a Kotlin file for your main program logic:

1. Right-click the **src** folder.
2. Select **New > Kotlin File/Class**.
3. Name the file `Main`.

Step 2: Understanding 3D Space

In AR, 3D space is represented by x, y, and z coordinates:

- **x**: Horizontal axis.
- **y**: Vertical axis.
- **z**: Depth (positive values are further away; negative are closer).

For this project, we will simulate object placement using these coordinates.

Step 3: Coding the 3D Space Logic

3.1 Define a Data Class for 3D Objects

A `data class` in Kotlin is perfect for representing an object with properties.

kotlin

```
// Represents a 3D object in
space
```

```kotlin
data class ARObject(

    val     name:        String,
// Object name

    var     x:           Float,
// X-coordinate

    var     y:           Float,
// Y-coordinate

    var     z:           Float
// Z-coordinate

) {

    // Move the object to a
new position

    fun  moveTo(newX:  Float,
newY: Float, newZ: Float) {

        x = newX

        y = newY
```

```
        z = newZ

    }



    // Print object's current
position

    fun printPosition() {

        println("$name        is
located at (x: $x, y: $y, z:
$z)")

    }

}
```

3.2 Define a Function for Object Placement

We will write a function to simulate placing objects in 3D space.

kotlin

```kotlin
fun placeObject(name: String,
x: Float, y: Float, z:
Float): ARObject {

    val obj = ARObject(name,
x, y, z)

    println("${obj.name}
placed at (x: ${obj.x}, y:
${obj.y}, z: ${obj.z})")

    return obj

}
```

Step 4: Adding Interactivity

We'll allow the user to:

1. Place objects.
2. Move objects.
3. List all objects.

4.1 Maintain a List of Objects

Use a mutable list to track all objects in the scene.

kotlin

```
val        objects        =
mutableListOf<ARObject>()
```

4.2 Create a Menu for User Interaction

Provide a menu-driven interface to interact with the app.

kotlin

```
fun showMenu() {

    println("\nSelect        an
action:")

    println("1.  Place  a  new
object")

    println("2.     Move     an
existing object")

    println("3.    List    all
objects")

    println("4. Exit")

}
```

4.3 Handle User Choices

Implement logic to handle each menu option.

kotlin

```kotlin
fun main() {
    println("Welcome to AR Object Simulator!")

    while (true) {
        showMenu()
        print("Enter your choice: ")
        when (readLine()?.toIntOrNull()) {
            1 -> {
```

```kotlin
        print("Enter
object name: ")
        val    name    =
readLine()!!
        print("Enter
x-coordinate: ")
        val    x    =
readLine()?.toFloatOrNull()
?: 0f
        print("Enter
y-coordinate: ")
        val    y    =
readLine()?.toFloatOrNull()
?: 0f
        print("Enter
z-coordinate: ")
```

```kotlin
                val    z    =
readLine()?.toFloatOrNull()
?: 0f


                val  newObject
= placeObject(name, x, y, z)

objects.add(newObject)
            }
            2 -> {
                if
(objects.isEmpty()) {

println("No objects available
to move.")
                    continue
            }
```

```kotlin
println("Available objects:")

objects.forEachIndexed           {
index,              obj              ->
println("${index         +         1}.
${obj.name}") }

            print("Select
object number to move: ")

            val   index   =
readLine()?.toIntOrNull()?.mi
nus(1)

            if  (index  ==
null       ||       index       !in
objects.indices) {

println("Invalid selection.")
```

```
                continue

            }


        print("Enter
new x-coordinate: ")

            val    newX    =
readLine()?.toFloatOrNull()
?: 0f

            print("Enter
new y-coordinate: ")

            val    newY    =
readLine()?.toFloatOrNull()
?: 0f

            print("Enter
new z-coordinate: ")
```

```kotlin
                val  newZ  =
readLine()?.toFloatOrNull()
?: 0f



objects[index].moveTo(newX,
newY, newZ)


println("${objects[index].nam
e} moved successfully.")
            }
            3 -> {

            if
(objects.isEmpty()) {

println("No  objects  placed
yet.")
```

```kotlin
        } else {

println("Current    objects    in
the scene:")

objects.forEach                {
it.printPosition() }
                }
        }
        4 -> {

println("Exiting            the
simulator. Goodbye!")
                break
        }
```

```
        else                    ->
println("Invalid          choice.
Please try again.")

            }

        }

}
```

Step 5: Running the Program

To test the program:

1. Run the `main.kt` file.
2. Use the menu to:
   - Place new objects in 3D space.
   - Move existing objects to new coordinates.
   - List all objects and their positions.

Example Run

mathematica

```
Welcome      to      AR      Object
Simulator!


Select an action:

1. Place a new object

2. Move an existing object

3. List all objects

4. Exit

Enter your choice: 1

Enter object name: Cube

Enter x-coordinate: 0

Enter y-coordinate: 1
```

Enter z-coordinate: -2

Cube placed at (x: 0.0, y: 1.0, z: -2.0)

Select an action:

1. Place a new object

2. Move an existing object

3. List all objects

4. Exit

Enter your choice: 3

Current objects in the scene:

Cube is located at (x: 0.0, y: 1.0, z: -2.0)

Select an action:

```
1. Place a new object

2. Move an existing object

3. List all objects

4. Exit

Enter your choice: 2

Available objects:

1. Cube

Select object number to move:
1

Enter new x-coordinate: 3

Enter new y-coordinate: 2

Enter new z-coordinate: -1

Cube moved successfully.
```

Key Takeaways

This project demonstrates how AR concepts like object placement and transformations can be implemented programmatically. While simple, it mirrors the logic of real AR apps and lays the groundwork for working with more complex AR libraries like ARCore. By practicing these fundamentals, you will be well-prepared for building robust AR applications.

Chapter 4: Understanding ARCore Fundamentals

Augmented Reality (AR) development requires a robust framework, and ARCore by Google stands out as one of the most effective platforms. This chapter will take you through ARCore's core components, how it handles AR sessions, tracks motion and planes, and integrates 3D objects into an

AR environment. You'll also learn to create an AR app that detects surfaces and places virtual objects on anchors.

4.1 Setting Up ARCore and Understanding its Core Components

ARCore is Google's Augmented Reality framework that enables developers to build immersive AR experiences. To get started, you need to set up ARCore in your Android project and understand the foundational components that drive ARCore's capabilities.

This section will walk you through installing ARCore, integrating it into your project, and explaining its core components in a practical, beginner-friendly way.

Setting Up ARCore in Your Project

Prerequisites

Before diving into ARCore, ensure the following:

- **Android Studio**: Installed and configured with Kotlin support.
- **Compatible Android Device**: Your device should support ARCore. You can verify the device compatibility here.

Step 1: Add ARCore Dependency

To use ARCore in your app, include the ARCore library in your project. Open your app's `build.gradle` file and add the following:

groovy

```
dependencies {
    implementation
'com.google.ar:core:1.44.0'
```

```
// Use the latest version
available

}
```

Sync your project to download the dependency.

Step 2: Update Android Manifest

For ARCore to function, you must add permissions and specify AR features in the `AndroidManifest.xml` file.

Add Camera Permissions

ARCore uses the device's camera to detect the environment. Include this permission:

xml

```xml
<uses-permission
android:name="android.permiss
ion.CAMERA" />
```

Specify AR Features

Declare AR as a required feature:

xml

```xml
<uses-feature
android:name="android.hardwar
e.camera.ar"
android:required="true" />
```

Add ARCore Metadata

Indicate that your app supports ARCore:

xml

```
<application>

    <meta-data

android:name="com.google.ar.c
ore"

android:value="required" />

</application>
```

Step 3: Verify ARCore Availability

Check if ARCore is installed and supported
on the user's device:

kotlin

```
import
com.google.ar.core.ArCoreApk


fun
checkArCoreAvailability():
Boolean {

    return              when
(ArCoreApk.getInstance().chec
kAvailability(this)) {


ArCoreApk.Availability.SUPPOR
TED_INSTALLED -> true

        else -> false

    }

}
```

Use this method to prompt users to install ARCore if it's unavailable.

Understanding ARCore's Core Components

ARCore operates based on three primary capabilities that make AR experiences possible: motion tracking, environmental understanding, and light estimation.

---

1. Motion Tracking

Motion tracking allows ARCore to understand the device's position and orientation in the real world. This is achieved using the device's camera and internal sensors.

How It Works

ARCore continuously maps the environment while tracking the device's movement, creating a virtual "coordinate system."

Key Concepts

- **Pose**: Represents the device's position and orientation in 3D space.
- **SLAM**: Simultaneous Localization and Mapping, the algorithm behind motion tracking.

Example: Retrieve the Device's Pose

kotlin

```
val           frame          =
arSession.update()

val pose = frame.camera.pose
```

```
// Extract position and
orientation

val x = pose.tx()

val y = pose.ty()

val z = pose.tz()

println("Device          position:
x=$x, y=$y, z=$z")
```

2. Environmental Understanding

ARCore detects flat surfaces in the environment, such as floors or tables, to place virtual objects realistically.

How It Works

The system scans for patterns using the camera feed to detect surfaces and calculates their boundaries.

Key Concepts

- **Planes**: Flat surfaces detected by ARCore.
- **Plane Extents**: Boundaries of the detected plane.

Example: Detect a Plane

kotlin

```
val          frame          =
arSession.update()

val          planes          =
frame.getUpdatedTrackables(Pl
ane::class.java)


for (plane in planes) {

    if    (plane.trackingState
== TrackingState.TRACKING) {
```

```
        println("Plane
detected:  ${plane.extentX}  x
${plane.extentZ}")

    }

}
```

---

3. Light Estimation

Light estimation allows ARCore to adjust the lighting of virtual objects to match the real environment, creating a seamless experience.

How It Works

ARCore analyzes the camera feed to determine the intensity and color of the ambient light.

Example: Retrieve Light Intensity

kotlin

```kotlin
val frame = arSession.update()

val lightEstimate = frame.lightEstimate


if (lightEstimate.state == LightEstimate.State.VALID) {

    val intensity = lightEstimate.pixelIntensity

    println("Ambient light intensity: $intensity")

}
```

Best Practices for ARCore Integration

1. **Optimize for Performance**: ARCore requires significant processing power. Avoid running unnecessary tasks in the main thread.
2. **Provide Fallbacks**: Always check for ARCore compatibility and offer alternative experiences for unsupported devices.
3. **Ensure User Consent**: Clearly explain why camera access is needed when requesting permissions.

4.2 ARCore Sessions and Configurations

ARCore sessions and configurations are the backbone of every augmented reality experience. An ARCore session manages the state and lifecycle of AR functionality, while configurations allow you to customize how the session operates, such as enabling plane detection, light estimation, or depth sensing.

In this chapter, we will explore what ARCore sessions and configurations are, how to set them up, and use them effectively to create rich AR experiences.

What is an ARCore Session?

An ARCore session represents the lifecycle of an AR interaction. When you start a session, ARCore initializes its sensors, camera, and environmental tracking. The session updates continuously to provide real-time information about the world.

Key Responsibilities of an ARCore Session

1. **Camera Management**: Access the camera feed and align it with AR elements.
2. **Tracking**: Monitor the device's position and orientation.
3. **Environment Understanding**: Detect planes, points, and light conditions.
4. **Session State**: Handle pause, resume, and reset operations for the AR experience.

Setting Up an ARCore Session

Step 1: Create and Start a Session

To start an AR session, initialize an instance of Session in your activity.

Code Example: Initializing a Session

kotlin

```kotlin
import
com.google.ar.core.Session


lateinit    var    arSession:
Session


fun initializeArSession() {
    try {

        arSession            =
Session(this)  //  Pass  the
context

        arSession.resume()  //
Start the session
```

```
    println("AR    session
started.")

  } catch (e: Exception) {

    println("Failed      to
start        AR        session:
${e.localizedMessage}")

  }
}
```

- **Session(this)**: Creates a session tied to the activity.
- **resume()**: Activates the session to start tracking.

Step 2: Handle the Session Lifecycle

It is crucial to manage the session lifecycle by pausing and resuming it when the activity is paused or resumed.

Lifecycle Management Example

kotlin

```kotlin
override fun onResume() {

    super.onResume()

    try {

        if
(::arSession.isInitialized) {


arSession.resume() // Resume
session

        }
```

```kotlin
        } catch (e: Exception) {
            println("Error
resuming        AR        session:
${e.localizedMessage}")
        }
    }


    override fun onPause() {
        super.onPause()
        if
(::arSession.isInitialized) {
            arSession.pause()    //
Pause session
        }
    }
```

What are ARCore Configurations?

Configurations customize how ARCore operates. For example, you can enable plane detection to place objects on flat surfaces or use depth sensing for more accurate placement.

Key Configuration Options

1. **Plane Detection**: Enables horizontal or vertical surface detection.
2. **Light Estimation**: Adjusts virtual objects based on ambient light.
3. **Depth API**: Provides advanced environmental understanding for occlusion and depth mapping.

Customizing ARCore Configurations

ARCore uses `Config` to define how a session behaves. You can modify configurations to suit your app's requirements.

Step 1: Create a Config Object

Use the `Config` class to define session behavior.

Code Example: Setting Up a Config

kotlin

```
import
com.google.ar.core.Config


fun configureArSession() {

    val       config       =
Config(arSession)

        config.planeFindingMode =
Config.PlaneFindingMode.HORIZ
```

```
ONTAL_AND_VERTICAL  //  Detect
planes


config.lightEstimationMode  =
Config.LightEstimationMode.EN
VIRONMENTAL_HDR  //  Advanced
light estimation


arSession.configure(config)
// Apply configuration

    println("AR         session
configured.")

}
```

Step 2: Enable Depth API (Optional)

For advanced AR features, such as occlusion
and realistic depth, enable the Depth API.

Code Example: Enabling Depth API

kotlin

```
config.depthMode          =
Config.DepthMode.AUTOMATIC

arSession.configure(config)
// Apply depth configuration

println("Depth API enabled.")
```

Step 3: Check Configuration Compatibility

Always validate whether the desired configuration is supported on the user's device.

298

Validation Example

kotlin

```kotlin
if
(!arSession.isDepthModeSuppor
ted(Config.DepthMode.AUTOMATI
C)) {

    println("Depth API is not
supported on this device.")

} else {

    config.depthMode        =
Config.DepthMode.AUTOMATIC


arSession.configure(config)

}
```

Session Update and Rendering

To receive updates from the session, call `session.update()` in your render loop. This retrieves the latest frame data, including tracking, planes, and light estimation.

Code Example: Updating the Session

kotlin

```
fun updateFrame() {

    val        frame        =
arSession.update() // Get the
latest frame

    val camera = frame.camera
```

```
    // Log the current camera
position

    val pose = camera.pose

    println("Camera position:
x=${pose.tx()},
y=${pose.ty()},
z=${pose.tz()}")

}
```

Call this method within a continuous loop, such as in a rendering thread.

Best Practices for ARCore Sessions and Configurations

1. **Optimize Performance**: Avoid unnecessary session updates or excessive configuration changes.

2. **Provide Fallbacks**: Handle devices that do not support specific configurations, like Depth API.
3. **User Feedback**: Notify users about required permissions or missing features.
4. **Reset Sessions When Necessary**: Allow users to reset the AR experience if tracking issues arise.

4.3 Working with ARCore Planes and Anchors

Working with planes and anchors is at the heart of creating interactive and immersive AR applications using ARCore. Planes allow ARCore to understand flat surfaces in the real world, while anchors help ensure that virtual objects remain accurately placed in the environment. This chapter will guide you through understanding, detecting, and managing planes and anchors, with practical examples to solidify your learning.

What Are ARCore Planes?

Planes represent real-world flat surfaces ARCore detects through its environmental understanding capabilities. For example, ARCore might detect a tabletop (horizontal plane) or a wall (vertical plane). These planes are dynamic; they adjust and grow as the AR session progresses, providing a robust spatial understanding.

Plane Types in ARCore

- **Horizontal Planes**: Flat surfaces like floors, tabletops, or ceilings.
- **Vertical Planes**: Upright surfaces such as walls or boards.
- **Arbitrary Planes**: Slanted or irregularly oriented surfaces (available with advanced configuration).

What Are Anchors?

An anchor in ARCore represents a fixed point in the physical world where virtual objects are placed. Anchors ensure that objects remain stable and accurately positioned even when the device moves or the camera view changes.

When you place a virtual object in your AR application, you attach it to an anchor to "tie" it to the real-world environment.

Detecting Planes

To work with planes, ARCore must continuously analyze the camera's view and sensors to identify surfaces.

Step 1: Enable Plane Detection

Plane detection is configured through the ARCore session's configuration.

Code Example: Enable Plane Detection

kotlin

```kotlin
import
com.google.ar.core.Config


fun
configurePlaneDetection(arSes
sion:
com.google.ar.core.Session) {

    val          config          =
Config(arSession)

        config.planeFindingMode   =
Config.PlaneFindingMode.HORIZ
ONTAL_AND_VERTICAL  //  Detect
```

```
horizontal     and      vertical
planes


arSession.configure(config)

    println("Plane    detection
enabled.")

}
```

Step 2: Retrieve Detected Planes

Planes are detected and updated with each
frame. You can access these planes via the
`Frame` object.

Code Example: Retrieve Planes

kotlin

```kotlin
import
com.google.ar.core.Plane

import
com.google.ar.core.Frame


fun retrievePlanes(arSession:
com.google.ar.core.Session) {

    val frame: Frame =
arSession.update()

    val planes =
frame.getUpdatedTrackables(Pl
ane::class.java)


    for (plane in planes) {

        if
(plane.trackingState ==
```

```
Plane.TrackingState.TRACKING)
{

        println("Plane
detected: ${plane.type}")

    }

  }

}
```

Handling Tap Events to Place Anchors

To make your AR app interactive, you can allow users to tap on the screen to place virtual objects on detected planes.

Step 1: Detect Tap Events

You need to listen for touch events and process them to identify valid hit results.

Code Example: Handling Tap Gestures

kotlin

```kotlin
import
android.view.MotionEvent

import
com.google.ar.core.HitResult


fun handleTapEvent(arSession:
com.google.ar.core.Session,
motionEvent: MotionEvent) {

    if (motionEvent.action ==
MotionEvent.ACTION_DOWN) {

        val        frame        =
arSession.update()

        val    hitResults    =
frame.hitTest(motionEvent)
```

```kotlin
for (hit in
hitResults) {

    val trackable =
hit.trackable

    if (trackable is
Plane &&
trackable.isPoseInPolygon(hit
.hitPose)) {

        val anchor =
hit.createAnchor()

println("Anchor created at:
${anchor.pose}")

        break
    }
}
```

```
        }

    }
```

Placing Virtual Objects

Once an anchor is created, you can attach a
virtual object to it. This often involves
integrating a 3D rendering engine like
Sceneform.

Step 1: Use Sceneform to Render Objects

Sceneform simplifies the process of
rendering 3D models on anchors.

Code Example: Attaching Virtual Objects

kotlin

```
import
com.google.ar.sceneform.Ancho
rNode

import
com.google.ar.sceneform.Node

import
com.google.ar.sceneform.rende
ring.ModelRenderable


fun
placeVirtualObject(anchor:
com.google.ar.core.Anchor,
sceneView:
com.google.ar.sceneform.Scene
View) {

    ModelRenderable.builder()
```

```kotlin
        .setSource(context,
R.raw.virtual_object_model)
// Replace with your 3D model

        .build()

        .thenAccept        {
modelRenderable ->

        val  anchorNode  =
AnchorNode(anchor).apply {

setParent(sceneView.scene)

        }
        val  objectNode  =
Node().apply {

        renderable  =
modelRenderable

setParent(anchorNode)
```

```
        }

        println("Virtual
object placed on anchor.")

        }

        .exceptionally        {
throwable ->

        println("Error
loading        3D        model:
${throwable.localizedMessage}
")

        null

        }

}
```

Understanding Anchor Management

Anchors are powerful but resource-intensive. It's important to manage them efficiently to maintain app performance.

Best Practices

1. **Limit the Number of Anchors**: Too many anchors can slow down your application.
2. **Remove Stale Anchors**: Use `detach()` to remove anchors no longer in use.
3. **Monitor Tracking Quality**: Validate the tracking state of planes and anchors periodically.

Code Example: Detaching Anchors

kotlin

```kotlin
fun        detachAnchor(anchor:
com.google.ar.core.Anchor) {

    anchor.detach()
```

```
    println("Anchor
detached.")

}
```

Key Takeaways

- Planes provide a foundation for placing virtual objects by detecting real-world surfaces.
- Anchors stabilize objects and tie them to the physical world.
- Efficient plane detection, anchor creation, and virtual object rendering are crucial for robust AR applications.

In the next section, we'll dive into how to integrate and manipulate 3D objects with ARCore. Stay tuned!

4.4 Integrating 3D Objects with AR in Android

In this chapter, we will explore how to integrate 3D objects into your ARCore-based Android app, allowing you to place and interact with virtual models in the real world. By the end of this chapter, you'll understand how to use 3D models, attach them to anchors, and display them in your AR environment. Let's get started!

Why 3D Objects in AR?

One of the most exciting aspects of AR development is the ability to overlay and interact with 3D objects in real-time. By placing 3D objects on real-world surfaces, we can create immersive experiences, such as virtual furniture in your living room, virtual characters, or even complex simulations.

ARCore, combined with Sceneform (a 3D rendering framework for Android), makes it straightforward to display and manipulate 3D objects in augmented reality.

Setting Up Sceneform for 3D Objects

Sceneform is a powerful tool that simplifies working with 3D models in AR. It abstracts away much of the complexity of handling 3D assets, making it easier to integrate objects into your AR scenes.

Step 1: Add Sceneform Dependencies

First, you'll need to include Sceneform dependencies in your project. Open your `build.gradle` (Module: app) file and add the following dependencies:

gradle

```
dependencies {

    implementation
'com.google.ar.sceneform:core
:1.17.1'

    implementation
'com.google.ar.sceneform.ux:s
ceneform-ux:1.17.1'

    // Optional: If you want
to load 3D models from glTF
files

    implementation
'com.google.ar.sceneform:scen
eform-assets:1.17.1'

}
```

Sync your project after adding these dependencies.

Step 2: Load a 3D Model

Now, let's load a 3D model into your app. Sceneform supports a variety of 3D model formats, such as `.obj`, `.fbx`, and `.gltf`. For simplicity, let's use a `.glb` file, which is a binary version of `.gltf`. You can download 3D models from sites like Google Poly, Sketchfab, or other 3D asset repositories.

For this tutorial, let's assume we have a model called `virtual_object.glb` stored in the `assets` folder of your Android project.

Step 3: Create an Anchor to Place the Model

Before you can render your 3D object, you need to create an anchor on a plane detected by ARCore. You can do this by using a tap gesture to select a point on the detected surface and then place the object there.

Here's how to detect the tap gesture and create an anchor at the selected point:

kotlin

```
import
android.view.MotionEvent

import
com.google.ar.core.HitResult

import
com.google.ar.core.Plane

import
com.google.ar.sceneform.Ancho
rNode

import
com.google.ar.sceneform.Node

import
com.google.ar.sceneform.rende
ring.ModelRenderable
```

```kotlin
import
com.google.ar.sceneform.ux.Ar
Fragment


fun onTap(event: MotionEvent,
arFragment: ArFragment) {

    // Get the frame from the
AR session

    val        frame        =
arFragment.arSceneView.arFram
e

    val      hitResults      =
frame?.hitTest(event)


    for (hit in hitResults!!)
{
```

```kotlin
        val    trackable    =
hit.trackable

        if    (trackable    is
Plane                       &&
trackable.isPoseInPolygon(hit
.hitPose)) {

            val    anchor    =
hit.createAnchor()


            // Place the 3D
model on the anchor

placeObject(arFragment,
anchor)
            break
        }
    }
```

```kotlin
}


fun placeObject(arFragment:
ArFragment, anchor:
com.google.ar.core.Anchor) {

    // Load the 3D model

    ModelRenderable.builder()


.setSource(arFragment.context
,
Uri.parse("model/virtual_obje
ct.glb"))

        .build()

        .thenAccept            {
renderable ->
```

```kotlin
        // Create a node
to hold the model and attach
it to the anchor

        val anchorNode =
AnchorNode(anchor)


anchorNode.setParent(arFragme
nt.arSceneView.scene)



        val modelNode =
Node()


modelNode.renderable      =
renderable


modelNode.setParent(anchorNod
e)

    }
```

```
        .exceptionally        {
throwable ->

            // Handle  model
loading failure

            Log.e("AR",
"Error    loading    model",
throwable)

            null

        }

}
```

Explanation of Code

- **onTap(event, arFragment)**: This
  function listens for tap gestures.
  When a user taps on the screen, it
  checks if the tap intersects with any
  detected planes. If a valid plane is

found, it creates an anchor at the hit location.

- **placeObject(arFragment, anchor)**: This function loads the 3D model from the `assets` folder using Sceneform's `ModelRenderable.builder()`. Once the model is loaded, it creates a `Node` to hold the model and attaches it to the anchor. The node is then added to the scene.

Interacting with 3D Objects

Once the 3D object is placed on the surface, it can be interacted with. You can rotate, scale, or move the object, allowing users to manipulate the virtual object in real-time.

Step 4: Adding Interactivity

To add simple interactivity, such as rotating the object, you can use gestures like drag or swipe. Here's an example of how you might rotate the 3D object with swipe gestures:

kotlin

```
fun     onRotateGesture(event:
MotionEvent, node: Node) {

    val deltaX = event.rawX

    val deltaY = event.rawY


    // Update the rotation of
the node

    node.localRotation      =
node.localRotation           *
Quaternion.axisAngle(Vector3(
0f, 1f, 0f), deltaX)

    node.localRotation      =
node.localRotation           *
```

```
Quaternion.axisAngle(Vector3(
1f, 0f, 0f), deltaY)

}
```

In this example, the rotation of the 3D object is updated based on the user's swipe movements.

Best Practices for 3D Model Integration

When working with 3D objects in AR, it's essential to keep performance in mind. Here are a few tips:

1. **Optimize Your 3D Models**: Ensure your 3D models are not too complex or too high-poly. Simplify models to maintain good performance.
2. **Use Low-Resolution Textures**: High-resolution textures can consume more memory and slow down the rendering process.

3. **Use Model LOD (Level of Detail)**: For complex scenes, consider using LOD to switch between detailed models and simplified ones depending on the user's distance from the object.

Key Takeaways

- **Sceneform** is a great library for rendering 3D models in AR, providing a simple interface to work with.
- **Anchors** are essential for placing virtual objects in the real world, and they can be attached to detected planes.
- **Interactivity** with 3D objects enhances the user experience by allowing them to manipulate objects in real-time.

- **Optimization** is crucial when working with 3D assets in AR to ensure a smooth user experience.

4.5 ARCore's Environment and Motion Tracking

In this chapter, we will explore the key components of ARCore's environment and motion tracking. Understanding how ARCore tracks the environment and how it handles the motion of devices in space is crucial for creating seamless and realistic AR experiences.

By the end of this chapter, you'll have a deeper understanding of how ARCore detects surfaces, tracks motion, and integrates this data into your augmented reality applications.

Understanding ARCore's Motion Tracking

Motion tracking is one of the cornerstones of augmented reality. Without it, your AR content would just float aimlessly in space, or worse, disappear as soon as you move your device.

ARCore's motion tracking relies on the camera and sensors in the device to detect how the device moves and how it relates to the physical world. ARCore uses a combination of visual features and device sensors to track the device's position and orientation in 3D space.

How Motion Tracking Works

ARCore's motion tracking works through these key elements:

1. **Feature Points**: ARCore detects features in the environment using the camera feed. These are the visual

features that the system uses to track movement.

2. **Inertial Sensors**: These sensors (accelerometer, gyroscope, etc.) provide data about the device's movement, helping ARCore refine its understanding of the device's position even when there are fewer visual features to track.

3. **SLAM (Simultaneous Localization and Mapping)**: ARCore employs a technique called SLAM to continuously track the device's position relative to its surroundings. It builds a map of the environment as it moves and uses that map to determine where the device is in space.

Step 1: Setting Up Motion Tracking in ARCore

To get started with motion tracking, we first need to set up an `ArFragment`, which will manage the AR session. This fragment automatically handles much of the motion tracking for us, including plane detection and surface tracking.

kotlin

```kotlin
// In your activity or fragment
class MainActivity : AppCompatActivity() {

    private lateinit var arFragment: ArFragment


    override fun onCreate(savedInstanceState: Bundle?) {

        super.onCreate(savedInstanceS tate)
```

```
setContentView(R.layout.activ
ity_main)


        arFragment         =
supportFragmentManager.findFr
agmentById(R.id.ux_fragment)
as ArFragment

    }

}
```

This fragment provides everything you need to get started with motion tracking and ARCore's camera feed. It automatically detects planes and sets up motion tracking.

Step 2: Understanding the Role of the Camera Feed

ARCore uses the device's camera to detect features in the environment. These features, such as edges or corners, help ARCore understand where the device is relative to the environment.

You don't need to worry about manually accessing the camera, as ARCore abstracts this for you. However, you can still interact with the camera feed directly if needed by accessing the arSceneView object.

For example, if you wanted to show a custom camera feed:

kotlin

```kotlin
val camera = arFragment.arSceneView.scene.camera

camera.position = Vector3(0f, 0f, -1f) // Position the camera at a set distance
```

This will allow you to control the perspective of the camera within your AR world.

Step 3: Tracking Motion with ARCore

ARCore's motion tracking allows the system to detect and react to movement. It's essential for placing objects in the world as the user moves the device.

ARCore uses `CameraPose` to track the camera's position and orientation. A `Pose` is simply the position and rotation of the device in 3D space, which is updated as the device moves.

You can get the current pose from the AR session like so:

kotlin

```
val          frame          =
arFragment.arSceneView.arFram
e

val          cameraPose          =
frame?.camera?.pose
```

With the `cameraPose`, you can track how the device is moving and orient objects accordingly.

ARCore's Environmental Understanding

While motion tracking tells us where the device is, **environmental understanding** allows ARCore to detect flat surfaces, like tables or floors, where virtual objects can be placed.

Step 4: Plane Detection

To place objects realistically in AR, ARCore needs to detect horizontal or vertical surfaces. This is done through **plane detection**. ARCore tracks the environment and looks for flat surfaces like tables, floors, or walls where objects can be placed.

You can enable plane detection in your AR fragment with the following code:

kotlin

```
arFragment.arSceneView.planeR
enderer.isEnabled = true

arFragment.planeDiscoveryCont
roller.setInstructionView(vie
w)
```

This code enables plane detection, allowing the user to view the surfaces that ARCore detects. The PlaneRenderer will render a visualization of detected planes, and the PlaneDiscoveryController will allow users to interact with the detected surfaces.

Step 5: Using Detected Planes for Object Placement

Once ARCore detects a plane, you can place virtual objects on it. This is done by creating an Anchor at the location of the plane and then attaching a 3D model to that anchor.

kotlin

```
val              frame          =
arFragment.arSceneView.arFram
e

val          hitResults        =
frame?.hitTest(event)
```

```
for (hit in hitResults!!) {

    val        trackable       =
hit.trackable

    if (trackable is Plane &&
trackable.isPoseInPolygon(hit
.hitPose)) {

        val        anchor       =
hit.createAnchor()


placeObject(arFragment,
anchor)

        break

    }

}
```

This code listens for tap gestures, detects where a user taps on the plane, and places an object at that location.

Motion and Environmental Feedback

One of the most compelling features of ARCore is the ability to combine motion tracking and environmental feedback. As the device moves, ARCore continuously updates its understanding of the world, making sure virtual objects are correctly placed and oriented relative to the real environment.

This is a core principle of AR: virtual objects must feel like they exist within the real world. Motion tracking ensures that they stay attached to the correct position, while environmental understanding makes sure they land on solid surfaces.

Step 6: Real-time Feedback for Users

To enhance the user experience, you can provide visual feedback. For example, you might want to show a grid or an outline where the object will be placed. This helps users interact with the AR content more intuitively.

kotlin

```
val          anchorNode          =
AnchorNode(anchor)

anchorNode.setParent(arFragme
nt.arSceneView.scene)


val modelNode = Node()

modelNode.renderable          =
renderable

modelNode.setParent(anchorNod
e)
```

Here, we place the 3D model on the detected surface and link it to the anchor. The model now follows the motion of the device, staying anchored to the surface.

Hands-On Project: Develop an App to Detect Surfaces and Place Virtual Objects on Anchors

In this hands-on project, we will develop an Android app that detects flat surfaces and places virtual 3D objects on them using ARCore. This project will cover essential concepts like surface detection, anchor creation, and object placement. We'll also work through code implementation step by step, so both beginners and experienced developers can follow along and build their understanding of ARCore.

By the end of this project, you'll be able to create an app where users can interact with virtual objects in the real world by simply tapping on detected surfaces.

Prerequisites

Before we start coding, ensure you have the following:

- **Android Studio**: This is the official IDE for Android development.
- **ARCore**: We will be using ARCore for augmented reality functionality.
- **Kotlin**: The project will be developed using Kotlin, the recommended language for Android development.
- **A physical device**: ARCore apps require a physical device to work, as emulators do not support AR features.

Step 1: Setting Up Your Project

Let's start by setting up a new Android project in Android Studio:

1. **Create a new project** in Android Studio.
   - Choose **Empty Activity**.
   - Set the **language** to **Kotlin**.
   - Set the minimum SDK to **API 24** or higher (since ARCore requires at least Android 7.0, API 24).

Add ARCore dependencies: Open the build.gradle (Module: app) file and add the following dependencies to enable ARCore in your project: gradle

```
dependencies {

    implementation
'com.google.ar:core:1.31.0'
```

```
    implementation
'com.google.ar.sceneform.ux:s
ceneform-ux:1.17.1'

}
```

2. Then sync the project to download the
   dependencies.

Step 2: Configuring ARFragment

We will use the `ArFragment` class from
ARCore, which simplifies most of the heavy
lifting in AR development. It automatically
handles the camera feed, motion tracking,
and plane detection for us.

Update your layout file
(`activity_main.xml`):
Replace the content of
`activity_main.xml` with the following
code to set up the ARFragment:
xml

```xml
<?xml version="1.0"
encoding="utf-8"?>

<RelativeLayout
xmlns:android="http://schemas
.android.com/apk/res/android"


android:layout_width="match_p
arent"


android:layout_height="match_
parent">




<com.google.ar.sceneform.ux.A
rFragment

android:id="@+id/ux_fragment"
```

```xml
    android:layout_width="match_p
    arent"

    android:layout_height="match_
    parent" />

</RelativeLayout>
```

1.

Configure the `ArFragment` in your `MainActivity`:

In `MainActivity.kt`, initialize the `ArFragment` to manage ARCore's session. kotlin

```kotlin
import android.os.Bundle

import
androidx.appcompat.app.AppCom
patActivity
```

```kotlin
import
com.google.ar.sceneform.ux.Ar
Fragment


class        MainActivity      :
AppCompatActivity() {

    private    lateinit    var
arFragment: ArFragment


    override              fun
onCreate(savedInstanceState:
Bundle?) {

super.onCreate(savedInstanceS
tate)

setContentView(R.layout.activ
ity_main)
```

```
        arFragment        =
supportFragmentManager.findFr
agmentById(R.id.ux_fragment)
as ArFragment

    }

}
```

2. This sets up the ARFragment and
   prepares it to manage the AR session.

Step 3: Detecting Surfaces

Now we'll implement the functionality to
detect surfaces (such as tables or floors) and
place virtual objects on them. ARCore will
automatically detect these surfaces, but we
need to respond to the detection events and
add our 3D object.

Detecting Surfaces Using Tap Events

We will handle tap gestures on the screen and place virtual objects at the locations where the user taps on a detected surface.

Handle Tap Gestures: Add the following code in MainActivity.kt to capture tap events and place objects on the detected surface: kotlin

```kotlin
arFragment.setOnTapArPlaneLis
tener { hitResult, plane,
motionEvent ->

    if (plane.type !=
Plane.Type.HORIZONTAL_UPWARD_
FACING) {


return@setOnTapArPlaneListene
r

    }
```

```
    // Create an anchor at
the tapped location

    val        anchor        =
hitResult.createAnchor()


    // Place the object at
the anchor

    placeObject(arFragment,
anchor)

}
```

1. This code listens for tap gestures on
   the screen. When the user taps on a
   horizontal surface (like a floor or
   table), it creates an anchor at the
   tapped location and places a virtual
   object there.

Step 4: Placing a Virtual Object

We need to load a 3D object and place it on the detected surface. Let's use a simple 3D model to demonstrate this. You can download a 3D model in `.glb` or `.obj` format from resources like Google Poly or any other 3D asset provider.

1. **Add 3D Model to Your Project**:
   Place the 3D model file in the `assets` folder of your Android project (create the folder if it doesn't exist).

Load and Place the 3D Object:
In `MainActivity.kt`, add a function to load and place the 3D model at the anchor:
kotlin

```
private                      fun
placeObject(arFragment:
ArFragment, anchor: Anchor) {

    // Load  the  model  from
the assets folder
```

```
ModelRenderable.builder()

    .setSource(this,
Uri.parse("model.glb"))

    .build()

    .thenAccept            {
modelRenderable ->

        // Create a Node
to attach the model

        val modelNode    =
Node()


modelNode.renderable       =
modelRenderable


modelNode.setParent(arFragmen
t.arSceneView.scene)
```

355

```kotlin
        // Create an
anchor node to attach the
object to the surface

        val anchorNode =
AnchorNode(anchor)


anchorNode.setParent(arFragme
nt.arSceneView.scene)


modelNode.setParent(anchorNod
e)

    }

    .exceptionally {

        // Handle the
case where model loading
fails

Toast.makeText(this,    "Error
```

```
loading                    model",
Toast.LENGTH_SHORT).show()


return@exceptionally null

        }

}
```

2. This function loads the 3D model, creates a Node to hold the model, and attaches it to the AnchorNode created earlier. This effectively places the model at the tapped location in the AR scene.

Step 5: Testing Your AR App

Before running the app, ensure the following:

- **ARCore** is installed on your physical device. You can download it from the Play Store if it's not already installed.

Camera Permissions are granted in your app. You can add these in the `AndroidManifest.xml`:
xml

```
<uses-permission
android:name="android.permiss
ion.CAMERA" />
```

Once everything is set up, connect your device via USB, enable **developer mode** on the device, and hit **Run** in Android Studio.

When the app launches, you should see a camera feed. Tap on a flat surface (like a table or floor), and the 3D model should appear on the surface.

Step 6: Enhancing the User Experience

To enhance the user experience, you could add the following features:

Surface Visualizations: Display a grid or plane visualization where users can see detected surfaces in real-time. You can enable plane detection visualization like this:
kotlin

```
arFragment.planeDiscoveryCont
roller.visibility            =
View.VISIBLE
```

- **Object Scaling or Rotation**: Allow the user to scale or rotate the object by adding gesture recognizers.

Conclusion

In this project, you've learned how to:

- Set up an ARCore-based Android app.
- Detect flat surfaces like floors and tables.
- Place virtual 3D objects on those surfaces.

This is the foundation of any AR application. In the next chapters, we'll dive deeper into interactions, object manipulation, and optimizing performance for a better user experience.

Chapter 5: Building Your First AR App with Kotlin

In this chapter, we will build a simple augmented reality (AR) app using Kotlin. We will start by designing an app where users can place a 3D object on a flat surface in the real world, and interact with it by scaling and positioning it. We will also cover essential topics like handling user inputs, testing, debugging, and optimizing your app for better performance.

By the end of this chapter, you'll have a fully functional AR app that allows users to place, scale, and position 3D objects, with a focus on usability and performance.

5.1 Designing a Simple AR Object Placement App

In this section, we will walk through the process of designing a basic augmented reality (AR) app where users can place a 3D object in the real world by tapping on flat surfaces. We'll use ARCore to detect horizontal surfaces, such as tables and floors, and allow users to place virtual objects on them. This is one of the most common interactions in AR apps, and it forms the foundation for many AR applications, from virtual furniture placement to interactive learning tools.

Step 1: Setting Up the Project

Before we dive into designing the app, let's ensure that your development environment is set up correctly. We'll start by creating a new Android project and adding ARCore dependencies.

1.1 Create a New Project in Android Studio

1. Open **Android Studio** and create a new project.
2. Select **Empty Activity** and choose **Kotlin** as the programming language.

3. Name your project (e.g.,
   `ARObjectPlacementApp`), and
   set the **Minimum SDK** to **API level
   24** or higher, as ARCore requires this
   minimum SDK.

1.2 Add ARCore Dependencies

Once your project is set up, we need to
include ARCore in your `build.gradle`
file. ARCore provides the libraries necessary
to build AR experiences on Android
devices.

1. Open the `build.gradle` file in the
   `app` directory.
2. Add the following dependencies:

gradle

```
dependencies {

    implementation
'com.google.ar:core:1.31.0'
```

```
    implementation
'com.google.ar.sceneform.ux:s
ceneform-ux:1.17.1'

}
```

3. Sync the project after adding the
   dependencies.

1.3 Set Up ARCore Permissions

ARCore requires certain permissions, such
as camera access, to function correctly.
Open the `AndroidManifest.xml` file
and add the following permissions:

xml

```
<uses-permission
android:name="android.permiss
ion.CAMERA" />
```

```
<uses-feature
android:name="android.hardwar
e.camera" />

<uses-feature
android:name="android.hardwar
e.camera.autofocus" />


<application


android:usesCleartextTraffic=
"true"


android:theme="@style/Theme.M
aterialComponents.DayNight.No
ActionBar">

    ...

</application>
```

Step 2: Setting Up the AR Environment

Now that the project is ready, we will set up the AR environment by integrating `ARFragment`, which is a powerful component provided by ARCore that simplifies the process of creating AR experiences.

2.1 Add ARFragment to Your Layout

In this step, we will define the user interface (UI) and place an `ARFragment` inside it. `ARFragment` takes care of most of the AR setup, such as motion tracking, surface detection, and camera management.

Open your `activity_main.xml` and add the following layout code:

xml

```xml
<?xml version="1.0"
encoding="utf-8"?>

<RelativeLayout
xmlns:android="http://schemas
.android.com/apk/res/android"

android:layout_width="match_p
arent"

android:layout_height="match_
parent">


    <!-- ARFragment to manage
AR session -->


<com.google.ar.sceneform.ux.A
rFragment
```

```
android:id="@+id/ux_fragment"

android:layout_width="match_p
arent"

android:layout_height="match_
parent" />



</RelativeLayout>
```

2.2 Initialize ARFragment in Your Activity

Now that we've added the ARFragment to the layout, we need to initialize it in the activity. Open MainActivity.kt and add the following code to bind the ARFragment to the activity:

368

kotlin

```kotlin
import android.os.Bundle

import
androidx.appcompat.app.AppCom
patActivity

import
com.google.ar.sceneform.ux.Ar
Fragment


class      MainActivity       :
AppCompatActivity() {

    private    lateinit    var
arFragment: ArFragment
```

```kotlin
    override                        fun
onCreate(savedInstanceState:
Bundle?) {

super.onCreate(savedInstanceS
tate)

setContentView(R.layout.activ
ity_main)


    //        Find        the
ARFragment in the layout

    arFragment            =
supportFragmentManager.findFr
agmentById(R.id.ux_fragment)
as ArFragment

    }

}
```

This code simply initializes the `ARFragment` and sets it up to be used in the AR session.

Step 3: Detecting Surfaces and Placing a 3D Object

Now that the AR environment is set up, let's add the functionality to detect surfaces and place a 3D object when the user taps on the screen.

3.1 Set Up Tap Listener

We will set up a tap listener to capture user taps on horizontal surfaces (e.g., the floor or a table). When the user taps, the app will place a 3D object at the tapped location.

Add the following code to `MainActivity.kt`:

kotlin

```kotlin
arFragment.setOnTapArPlaneLis
tener { hitResult, plane,
motionEvent ->

    if    (plane.type    !=
Plane.Type.HORIZONTAL_UPWARD_
FACING) {


return@setOnTapArPlaneListene
r

    }


    // Create an anchor at
the tapped location
    val      anchor      =
hitResult.createAnchor()
```

```
    // Place the object at
the anchor

    placeObject(arFragment,
anchor)

}
```

In this code:

- We check if the plane is horizontal (such as a floor or table). If it is, we proceed to create an anchor at the tapped location.
- The `hitResult` contains the position where the user tapped, and we use it to create an `Anchor` object.

3.2 Load and Place a 3D Object

Next, we'll load a 3D object and place it on the anchor. We will use `ModelRenderable` from Sceneform to load a 3D model and place it in the AR scene.

First, make sure you have a 3D model file in your assets folder. For this example, we'll use a `.glb` file.

Now, let's define the `placeObject` function in `MainActivity.kt`:

kotlin

```
private                    fun
placeObject(arFragment:
ArFragment, anchor: Anchor) {

    // Load the 3D model from
assets

    ModelRenderable.builder()

        .setSource(this,
Uri.parse("model.glb"))
```

```kotlin
        .build()

        .thenAccept              {
modelRenderable ->

            // Create  a  Node
for the 3D model

            val   modelNode   =
Node()


modelNode.renderable          =
modelRenderable



            // Set  the  parent
to the AR scene


modelNode.setParent(arFragmen
t.arSceneView.scene)
```

```kotlin
            // Create an
AnchorNode and attach the
model to it

            val anchorNode =
AnchorNode(anchor)


anchorNode.setParent(arFragme
nt.arSceneView.scene)


modelNode.setParent(anchorNod
e)

        }

        .exceptionally {

            // Handle model
loading failure

Toast.makeText(this,    "Error
```

```
loading                    model",
Toast.LENGTH_SHORT).show()


return@exceptionally null

        }

}
```

Here's what happens in the code:

- We load the 3D model using
  `ModelRenderable.builder()`
  and specify the model file from the
  assets folder.
- Once the model is loaded, we create a
  `Node` and set the `renderable`
  property to the loaded model.
- We then attach the model to an
  `AnchorNode`, which links the model
  to the real-world location (the surface
  the user tapped).

Step 4: Running the App

At this point, we've set up the basic functionality for detecting surfaces and placing a 3D object on them. Let's run the app on a physical device, as ARCore requires a real camera to function properly.

1. Connect your Android device to your computer.
2. Run the app on the device.
3. Once the app is launched, point the camera at a flat surface (e.g., a table).
4. Tap on the surface to place a 3D object. The object should appear at the location where you tapped.

5.2 Setting Up User Input for AR Interactions

In this section, we will focus on enhancing the interaction capabilities of your AR app by setting up user input to manipulate AR objects. User interaction is key to a great AR experience. We'll explore how to handle different types of input, such as tap gestures for placing objects, drag gestures for moving objects, and pinch gestures for scaling. These interactive elements help users feel more in control of the AR content they see and interact with.

We will build on the previous chapter where we placed an object in AR, and now, we'll add user input to manipulate that object, making the AR experience much more interactive and engaging.

Step 1: Handling Tap Gestures for Object Placement

In the previous chapter, we created an app where users could tap on a flat surface to place an object. Now, we'll take that a step further by providing feedback when a user taps on a specific location, such as changing the color of an object to indicate that it was successfully placed.

1.1 Enhancing the Tap Interaction

In `MainActivity.kt`, we already set up the tap listener for placing objects on detected surfaces. Let's enhance that functionality by adding a visual cue when an object is successfully placed.

Here's the modified tap gesture code:

kotlin

```
arFragment.setOnTapArPlaneLis
tener { hitResult, plane,
motionEvent ->

    // Check if the plane is
horizontal (e.g., floor,
table)
```

```kotlin
    if      (plane.type      !=
Plane.Type.HORIZONTAL_UPWARD_
FACING) {


return@setOnTapArPlaneListene
r

    }



    // Create an anchor where
the user tapped

    val       anchor        =
hitResult.createAnchor()



    // Place the 3D object at
the anchor

    placeObject(arFragment,
anchor)
```

```
    // Change object color as
a visual cue

    changeObjectColor(anchor)

}
```

In this code:

- We first check if the detected plane is horizontal (which is ideal for placing objects).
- After creating the anchor at the tap location, we call `placeObject()` to load and place the 3D object.
- The `changeObjectColor()` function will be used to alter the color of the object, providing the user with feedback.

Step 2: Handling Drag Gestures for Moving Objects

Now that we can place objects, the next step is to allow users to drag them around. This will involve detecting the user's touch movements and updating the object's position accordingly. We'll use the `MotionEvent` class to capture touch events.

2.1 Implementing Drag Gesture

To move objects, we'll need to listen for drag gestures and update the position of the object accordingly. Here's how you can implement this:

kotlin

```
var          previousTouch:
MotionEvent? = null
```

```kotlin
arFragment.arSceneView.scene.
addOnUpdateListener          {
frameTime ->

    // If a touch event was
detected

    previousTouch?.let {

        val       touch      =
motionEvent

        // Calculate movement
delta

        val deltaX = touch.x
- it.x

        val deltaY = touch.y
- it.y

        //      Update     the
object's position based on
the drag movement
```

```
        moveObject(deltaX,
deltaY)

    }

    previousTouch              =
motionEvent

}
```

Here's what happens:

- We listen for any updates to the AR scene.
- When a touch event is detected, we calculate the movement delta between the previous touch and the current one.
- Then, the moveObject() function is responsible for moving the 3D object based on the calculated delta.

2.2 Moving the Object

In the `moveObject()` function, we will update the position of the 3D object based on the detected touch movement:

kotlin

```
private                    fun
moveObject(deltaX:       Float,
deltaY: Float) {

    // Use the delta values
to adjust the position of the
3D object in the AR scene

    modelNode.localPosition  =
modelNode.localPosition.apply
{

        this.x += deltaX

        this.y += deltaY
```

```
        }

}
```

The `moveObject()` function:

- Uses the delta values (`deltaX`, `deltaY`) to adjust the object's position on the X and Y axes.
- The object's position is updated by modifying the `localPosition` property of the `modelNode`.

Now, your users will be able to tap on the screen to place the object, and drag their finger to move it around.

Step 3: Handling Pinch Gestures for Scaling Objects

Scaling is another important interaction in AR. In this step, we'll enable users to pinch-to-zoom the 3D object. The gesture will allow users to make the object bigger or smaller depending on the distance between their fingers.

3.1 Implementing Pinch Gesture

To implement pinch-to-zoom, we'll use the ScaleGestureDetector class, which helps detect pinch gestures. We need to set up a ScaleGestureDetector to listen for pinch events.

kotlin

```
val   scaleGestureDetector   =
ScaleGestureDetector(this,
object                    :
ScaleGestureDetector.SimpleOn
ScaleGestureListener() {

    override              fun
onScale(detector:
```

```kotlin
ScaleGestureDetector?):
Boolean {

        detector?.let {

            val scaleFactor =
it.scaleFactor

scaleObject(scaleFactor)

        }

    return true

    }

})


arFragment.arSceneView.scene.
addOnUpdateListener          {
frameTime ->
```

```
scaleGestureDetector.onTouchE
vent(motionEvent)

}
```

In this code:

- We create a
  `ScaleGestureDetector`
  instance and override its `onScale()`
  method. This method will be triggered
  whenever the user pinches the screen.
- The `onScale()` method receives
  the scaling factor (how much the user
  is pinching or spreading their fingers).
- We pass this scale factor to the
  `scaleObject()` method.

3.2 Scaling the Object

Now, let's implement the
`scaleObject()` function to adjust the

scale of the 3D object based on the pinch gesture:

kotlin

```kotlin
private                    fun
scaleObject(scaleFactor:
Float) {

    // Adjust   the   object's
    scale   based   on   the   pinch
    gesture

    val        newScale      =
    modelNode.localScale.apply {

        this.x *= scaleFactor

        this.y *= scaleFactor

        this.z *= scaleFactor

    }

}
```

In the `scaleObject()` function:

- We modify the `localScale` of the object by multiplying it with the scaling factor obtained from the pinch gesture.
- This will increase or decrease the size of the 3D model depending on how far apart the user's fingers are.

Step 4: Putting It All Together

Now that we've handled tap, drag, and pinch gestures, your app should allow users to interact with the AR object in various ways. The full code in `MainActivity.kt` should now include:

- Tapping to place objects on horizontal surfaces.
- Dragging objects to move them around.

- Pinching to scale the objects.

This multi-touch interaction setup creates a more engaging and interactive AR experience for users.

5.3 Handling AR Object Scaling and Positioning

In this chapter, we'll focus on managing the size (scaling) and positioning of objects in your AR application. These functionalities are crucial for creating immersive and user-friendly AR experiences. Users need the ability to resize objects to fit their environment and reposition them accurately within the AR scene.

Let's break this down into simple steps, ensuring that both beginners and experts can follow along.

Understanding Scaling and Positioning in AR

1. Scaling

Scaling refers to resizing the virtual object in your AR scene. For instance, a virtual chair might need to be scaled up or down to match the real-world furniture.

2. Positioning

Positioning involves determining where in the AR environment an object is located. This could be done dynamically (using gestures like drag or motion detection) or programmatically (placing an object at a predefined position).

Step 1: Setting Up ARCore Object Manipulation

To enable scaling and positioning, we will leverage ARCore's capabilities and integrate user input via gestures.

1.1 Integrating ARCore and Sceneform

Make sure your project includes ARCore and Sceneform dependencies. If not already configured, update your `build.gradle` file:

gradle

```
dependencies {

    implementation
'com.google.ar.sceneform:scen
eform:1.17.1'

    implementation
'com.google.ar:core:1.37.0'

}
```

Sync your project to ensure all dependencies are downloaded.

Step 2: Scaling Objects

To scale objects dynamically, we'll implement a pinch-to-zoom gesture using ScaleGestureDetector.

2.1 Adding Gesture Detection

Create a ScaleGestureDetector in MainActivity.kt to listen for pinch gestures:

kotlin

```
private lateinit var
scaleGestureDetector:
ScaleGestureDetector
```

```kotlin
override                fun
onCreate(savedInstanceState:
Bundle?) {


super.onCreate(savedInstanceS
tate)


setContentView(R.layout.activ
ity_main)


    // Initialize the scale
gesture detector
    scaleGestureDetector    =
ScaleGestureDetector(this,
object                  :
ScaleGestureDetector.SimpleOn
ScaleGestureListener() {
```

```kotlin
        override              fun
onScale(detector:
ScaleGestureDetector):
Boolean {

        val scaleFactor =
detector.scaleFactor

adjustObjectScale(scaleFactor
)
        return true
    }

    })

}
```

2.2 Adjusting the Object's Scale

Implement the `adjustObjectScale()` function to resize the 3D model dynamically:

kotlin

```kotlin
private fun adjustObjectScale(scaleFactor: Float) {
    if (::modelNode.isInitialized) {
        val currentScale = modelNode.localScale

        val newScale = Vector3(
            currentScale.x * scaleFactor,

            currentScale.y * scaleFactor,
```

```
          currentScale.z    *
scaleFactor

          )

          modelNode.localScale
= newScale

     }

}
```

How It Works:

1. The `scaleFactor` is obtained from the `ScaleGestureDetector`.
2. The current scale is retrieved using `modelNode.localScale`.
3. A new scale is calculated by multiplying the current scale by the factor.
4. The new scale is applied to the `modelNode`.

Step 3: Positioning Objects

Positioning involves determining the X, Y, and Z coordinates of the object in the AR space. We will handle this using drag gestures.

3.1 Adding Drag Gesture Detection

Set up a listener for drag gestures. In ARCore, this can be done by detecting touch movements using `MotionEvent`.

kotlin

```kotlin
private var previousTouch:
MotionEvent? = null
```

```kotlin
override                     fun
onTouchEvent(event:
MotionEvent): Boolean {

    when (event.action) {

MotionEvent.ACTION_DOWN -> {

            previousTouch    =
event

        }

MotionEvent.ACTION_MOVE -> {

            val    deltaX     =
event.x   -   (previousTouch?.x
?: 0f)

            val    deltaY     =
event.y   -   (previousTouch?.y
?: 0f)
```

```
moveObject(deltaX, deltaY)

        previousTouch      =
event

        }

    }

    return
super.onTouchEvent(event)

}
```

3.2 Moving the Object

Now, implement the moveObject()
function to update the object's position:

kotlin

```kotlin
private fun
moveObject(deltaX: Float,
deltaY: Float) {

    if
(::modelNode.isInitialized) {

        val position =
modelNode.localPosition


modelNode.localPosition =
Vector3(

            position.x +
deltaX / 1000, // Adjust
sensitivity as needed

            position.y,

            position.z +
deltaY / 1000

        )
```

```
        }

}
```

Key Points:

- The `deltaX` and `deltaY` values determine how far the object should move on the X and Z axes.
- We divide these values by a factor (e.g., `1000`) to control the movement sensitivity.

Step 4: Combining Scaling and Positioning

Integrate both functionalities so that users can scale and position objects simultaneously. Update the `onTouchEvent()` method to include gesture detection for both scaling and dragging:

kotlin

```
override                    fun
onTouchEvent(event:
MotionEvent): Boolean {


scaleGestureDetector.onTouchE
vent(event) // Handle scaling

    when (event.action) {


MotionEvent.ACTION_DOWN -> {

            previousTouch    =
event

        }
```

```kotlin
MotionEvent.ACTION_MOVE -> {

            val    deltaX    =
event.x  -  (previousTouch?.x
?: 0f)

            val    deltaY    =
event.y  -  (previousTouch?.y
?: 0f)


moveObject(deltaX, deltaY)

            previousTouch    =
event

        }

    }

    return
super.onTouchEvent(event)

}
```

Now, users can interact with AR objects intuitively:

- Pinch to scale objects.
- Drag to reposition them.

Step 5: Testing and Fine-Tuning

1. **Run the App:** Place an object in your AR environment and test the scaling and positioning gestures.
2. **Fine-Tune Sensitivity:** Adjust the scaling and movement factors to ensure a smooth user experience.
3. **Add Visual Feedback:** Provide visual indicators (e.g., highlights or haptic feedback) to show users that they are interacting with the object.

5.4 Testing and Debugging Your AR App

Testing and debugging are essential steps in AR app development. A robust app requires rigorous testing to ensure accurate rendering of AR content and a seamless user experience. Debugging identifies and resolves issues that might impact performance or usability. This chapter will guide you through systematic testing and debugging practices tailored for AR applications.

Understanding the Importance of Testing in AR

Augmented Reality introduces unique challenges:

- **Real-world integration**: Virtual objects must align with real-world elements accurately.

- **Device variation**: Different devices have varying AR capabilities.
- **Environment sensitivity**: Performance varies in diverse lighting, surfaces, and motion scenarios.

Testing ensures your app adapts effectively to these variables.

Step 1: Testing Your AR App

1.1 Testing on Multiple Devices

AR apps often perform differently based on hardware and software configurations. Test on a range of devices:

- **High-end devices**: Test for optimal performance.
- **Mid-range/low-end devices**: Evaluate compatibility and performance drops.

- **Different OS versions**: Ensure compatibility with Android versions supported by ARCore.

How to Test Device Compatibility

Run this code snippet to check ARCore compatibility:

kotlin

```kotlin
val isSupported =
ArCoreApk.getInstance().check
Availability(this).isSupporte
d

if (isSupported) {

    Log.d("ARCore",    "Device
supports ARCore.")

} else {

    Log.e("ARCore",    "Device
does not support ARCore.")
```

```
}
```

1.2 Simulating Different Environments

Test your app in various environments:

- **Indoor and outdoor settings.**
- **Bright and low-light conditions.**
- **Flat and irregular surfaces.**

Tips for Environment Testing

Use ARCore's debug planes and anchors to visualize object placement:

kotlin

```
sceneView.planeRenderer.isVis
ible = true // Enable debug
plane visualization
```

1.3 Functional Testing

Focus on core features:

1. **Object placement**: Verify objects are anchored correctly.
2. **Scaling and positioning**: Test gestures for resizing and moving objects.
3. **Tracking stability**: Ensure objects don't drift or jitter as the camera moves.

1.4 Performance Testing

Measure frame rates, memory usage, and CPU load:

- Use **Android Profiler** in Android Studio.
- Look for frame rate drops below 30 FPS during interactions.

Step 2: Debugging AR Issues

2.1 Common AR Issues and Solutions

Issue	Cause	Solution
Objects not aligned	Poor surface detection	Improve lighting; use flat surfaces.
Object jittering	Unstable tracking	Reduce camera movement speed.

| App crashes | Memory leaks or unsupported devices | Optimize memory usage; validate device compatibility. |
| Laggy interactions | High computational load | Optimize 3D models and code. |

2.2 Using ARCore Debug Tools

Enable ARCore's debugging features for better insights:

Debug Mode for Planes and Anchors: kotlin

```
arFragment.arSceneView.planeR
enderer.isVisible = true //
Show detected planes
```

1.

Logging for Tracking Status:
kotlin

```kotlin
val trackingState = frame.camera.trackingState

Log.d("TrackingState", "Current state: $trackingState")
```

2.

2.3 Debugging with Android Studio

Android Studio provides tools to debug AR apps effectively:

- **Logcat**: Monitor runtime logs for errors or warnings.
- **Debugger**: Add breakpoints to identify code execution issues.
- **Profiler**: Analyze CPU, memory, and network usage.

416

2.4 Handling Crashes

Use a `try-catch` block to prevent crashes from unhandled exceptions:

kotlin

```kotlin
try {

    val         anchor        =
hitResult.createAnchor()

    placeObject(anchor)

} catch (e: Exception) {

    Log.e("ARDebug",    "Error
placing            object:
${e.message}")

}
```

2.5 Optimizing AR Models

3D models can be resource-intensive. Optimize them to reduce app lag:

- **Use lightweight models**: Convert high-polygon models to low-polygon ones using tools like Blender.
- **Compress textures**: Reduce texture file sizes without compromising quality.
- **Pre-load assets**: Use async tasks to preload models and avoid runtime delays.

Step 3: Automated Testing for AR Apps

While manual testing is crucial, automate repetitive tasks to save time.

418

3.1 Writing Unit Tests

Use JUnit for testing non-AR-specific logic:

kotlin

```
@Test

fun testScaleFactor() {

    val initialScale = 1.0f

    val scaleFactor = 2.0f

    val      expectedScale     =
initialScale * scaleFactor


assertEquals(expectedScale,
adjustScale(initialScale,
scaleFactor))

}
```

3.2 Using Espresso for UI Tests

Automate UI interactions like placing objects or scaling:

kotlin

```
onView(withId(R.id.placeButto
n)).perform(click())

onView(withId(R.id.scaleGestu
re)).perform(swipeUp())
```

Step 4: Finalizing Testing and Debugging

1. **Run multiple iterations**: Identify edge cases and improve stability.
2. **Gather user feedback**: Conduct beta testing with real users.
3. **Test updates**: Ensure app stability after each code update.

5.5 Optimizing Your App for Performance

Performance optimization is critical for AR apps. Poor performance can lead to laggy interactions, reduced tracking accuracy, and a subpar user experience. This chapter explores strategies to optimize your AR app for smooth operation on a variety of devices, ensuring an engaging and seamless user experience.

Why Optimization Matters in AR Apps

Augmented Reality apps are resource-intensive. They rely on:

- **Real-time processing**: Camera input, tracking, and rendering.
- **High computational load**: Rendering 3D objects and managing ARCore's tracking systems.
- **Device compatibility**: Varying performance capabilities across devices.

Without optimization, these factors can degrade app responsiveness and user satisfaction.

Step 1: Optimizing 3D Models and Assets

1.1 Use Lightweight Models

High-polygon 3D models can slow down rendering. Optimize them:

- **Decimation in Blender**: Reduce the number of polygons without losing visible detail.
- **Use low-poly models**: Choose models with fewer polygons designed for mobile apps.

1.2 Compress Textures

Textures often take up significant memory. Compress them:

- Use **tools like TinyPNG** for image compression.
- Convert textures to **compressed formats** like .ktx.

1.3 Preload Assets

Preloading assets prevents lag during runtime:

kotlin

```java
// Asynchronous preloading of
3D model

ModelRenderable.builder()

    .setSource(this,
Uri.parse("model.sfb"))

    .build()

    .thenAccept { renderable
->

        preloadedModel       =
renderable

    }

    .exceptionally           {
throwable ->

        Log.e("AR",       "Error
loading model", throwable)
```

```
    null

  }
```

Step 2: Improving AR Tracking Efficiency

2.1 Optimize Plane Detection

Plane detection can be resource-heavy. Limit it to specific types of planes:

kotlin

```
val        config      =
arFragment.arSceneView.sessio
n?.config
```

```
config?.planeFindingMode     =
Config.PlaneFindingMode.HORIZ
ONTAL    //    Detect    only
horizontal planes

arFragment.arSceneView.sessio
n?.configure(config)
```

2.2 Control Anchor Count

ARCore tracks all anchors, which can
burden the system. Remove unnecessary
anchors:

kotlin

```
for          (anchor         in
trackedAnchors) {
```

```
    anchor.detach()    //    Free
up resources

}

trackedAnchors.clear()
```

Step 3: Memory and CPU Optimization

3.1 Manage Memory Usage

Memory leaks can lead to app crashes. Use tools like **LeakCanary** to detect leaks:

Install   LeakCanary:
groovy

```
implementation
```

```
'com.squareup.leakcanary:leak
canary-android:2.10'
```

- Monitor and fix leaks identified in the logs.

3.2 Reduce CPU Load

Offload heavy computations to background threads:

kotlin

```
// Example of using a
background thread for heavy
computation

CoroutineScope(Dispatchers.De
fault).launch {

    val         result      =
performHeavyComputation()
```

```
withContext(Dispatchers.Main)
{

        updateUI(result)      //
Update UI on the main thread

    }

}
```

Step 4: Optimizing Rendering

4.1 Simplify Materials

- Use simple materials without complex shaders.
- Combine multiple textures into a single texture atlas to reduce rendering overhead.

4.2 Limit Draw Calls

Reduce the number of objects rendered simultaneously:

- Batch objects into a single mesh when possible.
- Use **culling techniques** to hide objects not visible to the camera.

Step 5: Testing for Performance

5.1 Use Android Profiler

Measure CPU, GPU, and memory usage during runtime:

- Open Android Studio → **View** > **Tool Windows > Profiler**.

430

- Run your app and monitor performance metrics.

5.2 Analyze Frame Rates

Ensure a consistent frame rate of **30 FPS or higher** for AR apps:

Use ARCore's FrameTime API to monitor:
kotlin

```kotlin
val frameTime = arSceneView.scene?.frameTime

Log.d("FrameTime", "Current frame time: $frameTime ms")
```

-

Step 6: Optimizing App Size

6.1 Use App Bundles

431

Android App Bundles generate optimized APKs for specific devices:

Enable app bundles in your build.gradle:
groovy

```groovy
android {
    bundle {
        density {
            enableSplit = true
        }
        abi {
            enableSplit = true
        }
    }
}
```

}

6.2 Remove Unused Assets

Eliminate unused models, textures, and libraries to reduce the app size.

Step 7: Optimize User Experience

7.1 Minimize Latency

Latency can disrupt AR interactions. Pre-process AR elements and use smooth animations.

7.2 Optimize for Different Devices

Test your app on:

- Low-end devices to identify performance bottlenecks.
- High-end devices to ensure optimal utilization of resources.

Step 8: Continuous Monitoring and Updates

Even after optimization:

1. Monitor user feedback for performance issues.
2. Update the app to include new ARCore features and improvements.

Performance optimization in AR apps requires a multi-faceted approach, balancing rendering quality, computational efficiency, and resource management. By following these strategies, you ensure your app delivers a smooth, responsive, and enjoyable AR experience, regardless of device or environment.

Chapter 6: Advanced AR Features with Kotlin

In this chapter, we dive deeper into advanced AR features, empowering you to create highly interactive, immersive, and efficient AR applications. By the end of this chapter, you'll be equipped to develop interactive apps, integrate gaming logic, and explore techniques for rendering and optimization.

6.1 Creating Interactive AR Apps:

Interactive AR applications bring the virtual world to life by allowing users to interact with augmented objects. In this section, you'll learn how to detect and process gestures like tapping, dragging, and scaling to make your AR apps more engaging.

Why Gesture Detection is Key

In AR, gestures bridge the gap between the user and virtual elements. By leveraging gestures, you can allow users to manipulate objects, add new ones, or interact in meaningful ways.

Setting Up Gesture Detection

Kotlin provides powerful tools to handle gestures in ARCore, including:

1. **Tap Gesture**: Detects single taps, typically used for object placement.
2. **Drag Gesture**: Enables moving objects across the screen.
3. **Pinch Gesture**: Allows scaling objects.

Step 1: Detecting a Tap Gesture

The most common interaction in AR apps is tapping to place objects.

Example Code: Tap to Place an Object

Set up a tap listener in your ARFragment:
kotlin

```kotlin
arFragment.setOnTapArPlaneLis
tener  {  hitResult,  plane,
motionEvent ->

    // Create  an  anchor  at
the tapped location

    val        anchor       =
hitResult.createAnchor()

    placeObject(anchor)

}
```

   1.

Implement the placeObject function:
kotlin

```kotlin
private                    fun
placeObject(anchor: Anchor) {
```

438

```kotlin
ModelRenderable.builder()

    .setSource(this,
Uri.parse("model.sfb"))      //
Replace with your 3D model

    .build()

    .thenAccept              {
renderable ->

        val   anchorNode   =
AnchorNode(anchor).apply {

            renderable   =
renderable

        }


arFragment.arSceneView.scene.
addChild(anchorNode)

    }
```

```
        .exceptionally          {
throwable ->

            Log.e("ARApp",
"Error      loading      model:
${throwable.message}")

            null

    }

}
```

2.
- **Explanation**:
  - The `onTapArPlaneListener` detects a user tap on a plane.
  - The `hitResult` provides the 3D location of the tap, and the anchor is created there.
  - The model is loaded and placed at the anchor's position.

Step 2: Adding Drag Gesture Support

Dragging allows users to reposition objects intuitively.

Example Code: Dragging Objects

Add a `TransformableNode` to enable manipulation:
kotlin

```kotlin
val transformationSystem =
TransformationSystem(resource
s.displayMetrics,
FootprintSelectionVisualizer(
))


val anchorNode =
AnchorNode(anchor)

val transformableNode =
TransformableNode(transformat
ionSystem).apply {
```

```
    setParent(anchorNode)

    renderable                =
modelRenderable   //   Your   3D
model

}

arFragment.arSceneView.scene.
addChild(anchorNode)

transformableNode.select()
```

1.
2. **Explanation**:
    - TransformationSystem handles interactions like dragging and scaling.
    - TransformableNode wraps the 3D object, making it interactable.

Step 3: Scaling with Pinch Gestures

Scaling objects is particularly useful in AR to adjust size for better visual context.

Example Code: Enabling Scaling

By default, `TransformableNode` supports scaling. To customize:

Set scaling properties:
kotlin

```
transformableNode.scaleContro
ller.minScale = 0.5f

transformableNode.scaleContro
ller.maxScale = 2.0f
```

1.
2. **Explanation**:
   - `minScale` ensures the object does not shrink below a usable size.
   - `maxScale` caps how large the object can grow.

443

Customizing Gesture Responses

To make your AR app truly interactive, you can customize gesture behavior.

Example Code: Responding to Tap Events

Display a toast message when an object is tapped:

Add a click listener:
kotlin

```
transformableNode.setOnTapLis
tener { _, _ ->

    Toast.makeText(this,
"Object                Tapped!",
Toast.LENGTH_SHORT).show()

}
```

1.

2. **Explanation**:
   - `setOnTapListener` captures taps on the object.
   - You can trigger any response, such as animations or API calls.

Best Practices for Interactive AR Apps

1. **Use Feedback**: Provide visual or haptic feedback for gestures to make the app feel responsive.
   - For example, use vibrations when an object is selected or scaled.
2. **Limit Complexity**: Avoid overloading users with too many gesture options at once. Start with basic interactions and layer complexity as needed.
3. **Test Interactions**: Ensure gestures work across different devices and screen sizes.

Final Example: Bringing It All Together

This example combines tap detection, object placement, and interaction:

kotlin

```kotlin
arFragment.setOnTapArPlaneLis
tener { hitResult, plane,
motionEvent ->

    val        anchor       =
hitResult.createAnchor()


    ModelRenderable.builder()

        .setSource(this,
Uri.parse("object_model.sfb")
)

        .build()
```

```kotlin
            .thenAccept              {
modelRenderable ->

            val   anchorNode   =
AnchorNode(anchor)

            val
transformableNode              =
TransformableNode(arFragment.
transformationSystem).apply {


setParent(anchorNode)

                renderable   =
modelRenderable


scaleController.minScale     =
0.5f


scaleController.maxScale     =
1.5f
```

```kotlin
            // Add a tap
listener for user feedback

setOnTapListener { _, _ ->

Toast.makeText(this@MainActiv
ity, "Object Interacted!",
Toast.LENGTH_SHORT).show()
            }
        }

arFragment.arSceneView.scene.
addChild(anchorNode)

transformableNode.select()
    }
```

```
            .exceptionally        {
throwable ->

              Log.e("ARApp",
"Model      loading      failed:
${throwable.message}")

              null

          }

    }
```

- **What this does**:
  - Taps on a plane create an anchor.
  - A 3D object is placed at the anchor.
  - The object can be dragged, scaled, and tapped for feedback.

6.2 Using AR for Gaming: Building a Basic AR Game

Augmented Reality (AR) games bring unique interactivity by blending the physical and digital worlds. In this chapter, you'll learn to create a basic AR game using Kotlin and ARCore. This game will challenge the player to tap on virtual objects to score points, introducing essential game mechanics like object spawning, collision detection, and scoring.

Game Overview

We'll develop a simple AR game where:

1. Virtual objects appear randomly on detected surfaces.
2. The player scores points by tapping on these objects.
3. The game has a timer and displays the final score at the end.

Step 1: Setting Up the Game Environment

To start, set up a new project with ARCore and Sceneform dependencies.

Adding Dependencies

Ensure your `build.gradle` file includes:

groovy

```
dependencies {

    implementation
'com.google.ar:core:1.42.0'

    implementation
'com.gorisse:sceneform:1.19.4
'

}
```

Initializing the AR Game

Set up the ARFragment and load a basic layout with a score display.

XML Layout

Create a layout file (`activity_main.xml`) for the game:

xml

```
<RelativeLayout
xmlns:android="http://schemas
.android.com/apk/res/android"


android:layout_width="match_p
arent"
```

```
android:layout_height="match_
parent">


    <!-- AR Fragment -->

    <fragment


android:id="@+id/arFragment"


android:name="com.google.ar.s
ceneform.ux.ArFragment"


android:layout_width="match_p
arent"


android:layout_height="match_
parent" />
```

```xml
<!-- Score Display -->

<TextView

android:id="@+id/scoreTextView"

android:layout_width="wrap_content"

android:layout_height="wrap_content"

android:layout_alignParentTop="true"

android:layout_margin="16dp"
```

```xml
        android:background="#AA000000
"

        android:padding="8dp"

        android:text="Score:
0"

        android:textColor="#FFFFFF"

        android:textSize="18sp" />


    <!-- Timer -->

    <TextView

        android:id="@+id/timerTextVie
w"
```

```xml
android:layout_width="wrap_co
ntent"

android:layout_height="wrap_c
ontent"

android:layout_alignParentTop
="true"

android:layout_alignParentEnd
="true"

android:layout_margin="16dp"

android:background="#AA000000
"

        android:padding="8dp"
```

```
        android:text="Time:
60"

android:textColor="#FFFFFF"

android:textSize="18sp" />

</RelativeLayout>
```

Step 2: Spawning Virtual Objects

In AR gaming, objects need to appear dynamically. Let's write code to randomly spawn objects on detected planes.

Loading the Object Model

First, prepare the 3D object model (sphere.sfb) and add it to the assets folder.

Code for Object Spawning

Add the following function in your `MainActivity`:

kotlin

```kotlin
private                      fun
spawnObject(anchor: Anchor) {
    ModelRenderable.builder()
        .setSource(this,
Uri.parse("sphere.sfb"))
        .build()
        .thenAccept               {
renderable ->
            val  anchorNode  =
AnchorNode(anchor).apply {
```

```
            renderable  =
renderable

            }


arFragment.arSceneView.scene.
addChild(anchorNode)


            //      Add      tap
listener for scoring


anchorNode.setOnTapListener  {
_, _ ->


arFragment.arSceneView.scene.
removeChild(anchorNode)


currentScore++
```

```
                updateScore()

            }

        }

        .exceptionally          {
throwable ->

            Log.e("ARGame",
"Error     loading     model:
${throwable.message}")

            null

        }

    }
```

Random Spawning

Use a timer to spawn objects at random
intervals.

Timer Implementation

kotlin

```kotlin
private                        fun
startSpawningObjects() {

    val        handler        =
Handler(Looper.getMainLooper(
))

    val runnable = object :
Runnable {

        override fun run() {

            if (remainingTime
> 0) {

                // Create a
random anchor for the object
```

```kotlin
            val hitResult
= getRandomPlaneHitResult()

            if (hitResult
!= null) {

                val
anchor                    =
hitResult.createAnchor()

spawnObject(anchor)

                }

handler.postDelayed(this,
2000) // Spawn every 2
seconds

            }

        }

    }
```

```
handler.post(runnable)

}
```

Step 3: Handling Scoring

Update the score when a player taps on an object.

Score Update

Add these variables:

kotlin

```
private var currentScore = 0

private var remainingTime = 60
```

Create a function to update the score display:

kotlin

```kotlin
private fun updateScore() {

    val scoreTextView =
findViewById<TextView>(R.id.s
coreTextView)

    scoreTextView.text =
"Score: $currentScore"

}
```

Step 4: Adding a Timer

A countdown timer adds urgency to the game.

Countdown Implementation

kotlin

```kotlin
private fun startTimer() {

    val     timerTextView    =
findViewById<TextView>(R.id.t
imerTextView)

    val        handler        =
Handler(Looper.getMainLooper(
))

    val runnable = object :
Runnable {

        override fun run() {

            if (remainingTime
> 0) {

remainingTime--
```

```
timerTextView.text   =   "Time:
$remainingTime"


handler.postDelayed(this,
1000) // Update every second
                } else {

                    endGame()

                }

            }

        }

        handler.post(runnable)

}
```

Step 5: Ending the Game

When the timer runs out, display the final score and disable further interaction.

Game Over Screen

kotlin

```kotlin
private fun endGame() {

    runOnUiThread {

AlertDialog.Builder(this)

            .setTitle("Game
Over")

            .setMessage("Your
final        score        is:
$currentScore")

.setPositiveButton("Play
```

```
Again") { _, _ -> resetGame()
}


.setNegativeButton("Exit")   {
_, _ -> finish() }

            .show()

    }

}
```

Resetting the Game

kotlin

```
private fun resetGame() {

    currentScore = 0

    remainingTime = 60
```

```kotlin
    updateScore()

    startTimer()

    startSpawningObjects()

}
```

Final Code Integration

In your onCreate method:

kotlin

```kotlin
override                          fun
onCreate(savedInstanceState:
Bundle?) {


super.onCreate(savedInstanceS
tate)
```

```
setContentView(R.layout.activ
ity_main)


    arFragment                =
supportFragmentManager.findFr
agmentById(R.id.arFragment)
as ArFragment


    startTimer()

    startSpawningObjects()

}
```

Testing the Game

1. **Environment Setup**:
   ○ Use a well-lit area with flat surfaces for best results.
   ○ Test on multiple devices to ensure consistency.
2. **Debugging**:
   ○ If objects don't appear, check your plane detection and 3D model paths.
   ○ Ensure the ARCore version matches your device's capabilities.

6.3 Advanced 3D Rendering Techniques with OpenGL and ARCore

Incorporating advanced 3D rendering techniques into AR applications is essential for creating visually impressive and immersive experiences. OpenGL is a powerful graphics library that enables detailed rendering, and when combined with

ARCore, it allows developers to integrate high-performance 3D graphics seamlessly into augmented reality applications.

This chapter delves into using OpenGL with ARCore to implement advanced rendering techniques, providing you with the knowledge and practical examples needed to create stunning AR visuals.

Why Use OpenGL in ARCore?

While ARCore handles plane detection, anchors, and environment tracking, OpenGL allows you to:

- Render custom 3D objects.
- Apply advanced lighting and shading effects.
- Manipulate vertex and fragment shaders for realistic rendering.

Setting Up OpenGL in an ARCore Project

To use OpenGL in your ARCore project, you must configure the rendering pipeline. Start by adding dependencies and setting up basic OpenGL components.

1. Add OpenGL Support

Ensure your project supports OpenGL ES 3.0:

xml

```
<uses-feature
android:glEsVersion="0x000300
00"    android:required="true"
/>
```

2. Create a Custom Renderer

The renderer will manage all OpenGL drawing operations.

CustomGLRenderer Class

kotlin

```
class    CustomGLRenderer   :
GLSurfaceView.Renderer {

    private              val
vertexShaderCode = """

        attribute         vec4
vPosition;

        void main() {

            gl_Position       =
vPosition;
```

```
        }
    """



    private                val
fragmentShaderCode = """

        precision          mediump
float;

        uniform vec4 vColor;

        void main() {

            gl_FragColor      =
vColor;

        }
    """
```

```kotlin
    private val vertices =
floatArrayOf(
        0.0f, 0.5f, 0.0f,
        -0.5f, -0.5f, 0.0f,
        0.5f, -0.5f, 0.0f
    )


    private var vertexBuffer:
FloatBuffer =

ByteBuffer.allocateDirect(ver
tices.size * 4)

.order(ByteOrder.nativeOrder(
))
            .asFloatBuffer()
```

```kotlin
            .apply              {
put(vertices).position(0) }


    private var program: Int
= 0


    override              fun
onSurfaceCreated(gl:    GL10?,
config: EGLConfig?) {


GLES20.glClearColor(0.0f,
0.0f, 0.0f, 1.0f)


        // Compile shaders
and link program
```

```kotlin
val vertexShader =
loadShader(GLES20.GL_VERTEX_S
HADER, vertexShaderCode)

val fragmentShader =
loadShader(GLES20.GL_FRAGMENT
_SHADER, fragmentShaderCode)

program =
GLES20.glCreateProgram().appl
y {

GLES20.glAttachShader(this,
vertexShader)

GLES20.glAttachShader(this,
fragmentShader)

GLES20.glLinkProgram(this)

}
```

```
    }


    override                fun
onDrawFrame(gl: GL10?) {


GLES20.glClear(GLES20.GL_COLO
R_BUFFER_BIT)



GLES20.glUseProgram(program)



        val  positionHandle  =
GLES20.glGetAttribLocation(pr
ogram, "vPosition")


GLES20.glEnableVertexAttribAr
ray(positionHandle)
```

```
GLES20.glVertexAttribPointer(

        positionHandle,
3,   GLES20.GL_FLOAT,   false,
12, vertexBuffer

        )



        val   colorHandle   =
GLES20.glGetUniformLocation(p
rogram, "vColor")


GLES20.glUniform4fv(colorHand
le,   1,   floatArrayOf(1.0f,
0.0f, 0.0f, 1.0f), 0)



GLES20.glDrawArrays(GLES20.GL
```

```
_TRIANGLES,  0,  vertices.size
/ 3)



GLES20.glDisableVertexAttribA
rray(positionHandle)

    }


    override            fun
onSurfaceChanged(gl:   GL10?,
width: Int, height: Int) {

        GLES20.glViewport(0,
0, width, height)

    }
```

```kotlin
    private                fun
loadShader(type:          Int,
shaderCode: String): Int {

       return
GLES20.glCreateShader(type).a
pply {


GLES20.glShaderSource(this,
shaderCode)


GLES20.glCompileShader(this)

       }

     }

   }
```

Combine OpenGL rendering with ARCore's session to overlay 3D content on detected surfaces.

Custom GLSurfaceView

Create a custom `GLSurfaceView` to host the renderer:

kotlin

```kotlin
class
CustomGLSurfaceView(context:
Context)                       :
GLSurfaceView(context) {

    private    val    renderer:
CustomGLRenderer


    init {
```

```
setEGLContextClientVersion(3)
// Use OpenGL ES 3.0

        renderer              =
CustomGLRenderer()

        setRenderer(renderer)

    }

}
```

Advanced Rendering Techniques

1. Lighting and Shadows

To add realistic lighting:

- Use Phong or Blinn-Phong shading in the fragment shader.
- Include normal vectors and light direction calculations.

484

Enhanced Fragment Shader

glsl

```glsl
precision mediump float;

uniform vec3 uLightDirection;
varying vec3 vNormal;

void main() {
    float   lightIntensity   =
max(dot(normalize(vNormal),
normalize(uLightDirection)),
0.0);
```

```
gl_FragColor               =
vec4(vec3(1.0,  0.5,  0.3)  *
lightIntensity, 1.0);

}
```

---

2. Texture Mapping

Textures enhance the visual appeal of 3D models.

Loading Textures

kotlin

```
private                    fun
loadTexture(resourceId:  Int):
Int {

    val     textureHandle     =
IntArray(1)
```

```kotlin
    GLES20.glGenTextures(1,
textureHandle, 0)


    if  (textureHandle[0]   !=
0) {

        val      bitmap      =
BitmapFactory.decodeResource(
context.resources,
resourceId)



GLES20.glBindTexture(GLES20.G
L_TEXTURE_2D,
textureHandle[0])


GLUtils.texImage2D(GLES20.GL_
TEXTURE_2D, 0, bitmap, 0)

        bitmap.recycle()
```

```
GLES20.glTexParameteri(


GLES20.GL_TEXTURE_2D,
GLES20.GL_TEXTURE_MIN_FILTER,
GLES20.GL_LINEAR

        )


GLES20.glTexParameteri(


GLES20.GL_TEXTURE_2D,
GLES20.GL_TEXTURE_MAG_FILTER,
GLES20.GL_LINEAR

        )

    }
```

```
   return textureHandle[0]

}
```

Step-by-Step Implementation: A Rotating Cube

1. Define Cube Vertices

Add vertices and texture coordinates for a cube.

2. Update Renderer

Modify the `CustomGLRenderer` to draw the cube and apply rotation.

Testing and Debugging

1. Test rendering on multiple devices to ensure compatibility.

2. Use OpenGL debugging tools like Android Studio's GPU profiler.

6.4 IoT and AR Apps

Augmented Reality (AR) and the Internet of Things (IoT) are a powerful combination. By integrating real-time IoT data with AR applications, developers can create immersive and interactive experiences. Whether it's visualizing sensor data in AR or controlling IoT devices through an AR interface, this fusion opens up endless possibilities.

This chapter focuses on connecting AR applications with IoT systems, processing real-time data, and rendering it meaningfully within the AR environment.

Key Concepts in IoT and AR Integration

1. **IoT Data Sources**: Devices like sensors, smart home gadgets, and industrial machines generate data that can be accessed via APIs or direct communication protocols like MQTT.
2. **AR Visualization**: AR provides a spatial context for data, such as displaying temperature readings above a thermostat or overlaying equipment status on machinery.
3. **Real-Time Updates**: IoT systems often produce dynamic data that must be processed and displayed promptly.

Setting Up the Project

To demonstrate real-time data integration, we'll build a Kotlin-based AR app that retrieves sensor data from an IoT device (simulated via a cloud API) and displays it in AR.

Dependencies

Ensure you add the following dependencies:

groovy

```groovy
dependencies {
    implementation
'com.google.ar:core:1.36.0'

    implementation
'org.eclipse.paho:org.eclipse
.paho.client.mqttv3:1.2.5'   //
For MQTT
```

```
    implementation
'com.squareup.retrofit2:retro
fit:2.9.0' // For API calls

    implementation
'com.squareup.retrofit2:conve
rter-gson:2.9.0'

}
```

---

1. Connect to IoT Data Source

Simulated IoT API

For this example, we simulate an IoT device by creating a cloud API endpoint that returns JSON data:

json

```
{
```

```
  "temperature": 23.5,

  "humidity": 60

}
```

Create a Retrofit API Interface

kotlin

```
interface IoTApi {

    @GET("sensor/data")

    suspend                 fun
getSensorData(): SensorData

}
```

```
data class SensorData(
```

```kotlin
    val temperature: Float,

    val humidity: Int
)
```

Initialize Retrofit

kotlin

```kotlin
val retrofit = Retrofit.Builder()

    .baseUrl("https://api.example.com/")

    .addConverterFactory(GsonConverterFactory.create())
```

```
.build()
```

```
val              api              =
retrofit.create(IoTApi::class
.java)
```

2. Fetch Real-Time Data

Use Kotlin coroutines to fetch data periodically:

kotlin

```
class    IoTDataFetcher(private
val api: IoTApi) {

    private    val    scope    =
CoroutineScope(Dispatchers.IO
)
```

```kotlin
fun
startFetching(onDataReceived:
(SensorData) -> Unit) {

    scope.launch {

        while   (isActive)
{

            try {

                val    data
= api.getSensorData()

withContext(Dispatchers.Main)
{

onDataReceived(data)

                }
```

```kotlin
                } catch (e:
Exception) {

e.printStackTrace()

                }

                delay(2000)
// Fetch data every 2 seconds

            }

        }

    }


    fun stopFetching() {

        scope.cancel()

    }

}
```

3. Display Data in AR

Render IoT Data in ARCore

Create an AR overlay that displays sensor data near a detected plane.

kotlin

```
class         IoTARActivity      :
AppCompatActivity() {

    private    lateinit    var
arFragment: ArFragment

    private    lateinit    var
dataFetcher: IoTDataFetcher
```

```kotlin
    override                    fun
onCreate(savedInstanceState:
Bundle?) {

super.onCreate(savedInstanceS
tate)

setContentView(R.layout.activ
ity_ar)


        arFragment          =
supportFragmentManager.findFr
agmentById(R.id.arFragment)
as ArFragment

        val         api        =
Retrofit.Builder()
```

```
.baseUrl("https://api.example
.com/")


.addConverterFactory(GsonConv
erterFactory.create())
            .build()


.create(IoTApi::class.java)


        dataFetcher          =
IoTDataFetcher(api)


dataFetcher.startFetching    {
data ->


updateArOverlay(data)
```

```kotlin
        }

    }


    private                        fun
updateArOverlay(data:
SensorData) {


arFragment.arSceneView.scene?
.apply {

        val     anchor     =
createAnchor()   //  Implement
logic  to  detect  or  use  an
existing anchor

        val      node      =
createNodeWithText("Temp:
${data.temperature}°C\nHumidi
ty: ${data.humidity}%")
```

```kotlin
            node.setParent(anchor)

                addChild(node)

            }

        }


    private                    fun
createNodeWithText(text:
String): Node {

        val node = Node()

        val    textView    =
TextView(this).apply {

            this.text = text

            textSize = 12f

setTextColor(Color.WHITE)
```

```kotlin
            setBackgroundColor(Color.argb
        (150, 0, 0, 0))

                }

            node.renderable        =
        ViewRenderable.builder()

                    .setView(this,
        textView)

                    .build()

                    .get()

            return node

        }


        private                    fun
        createAnchor(): Anchor {
```

```kotlin
        val        frame        =
arFragment.arSceneView.arFram
e ?: return null

        val        hitResult        =
frame.hitTest(0.5f,
0.5f).firstOrNull { hit ->

            hit.trackable    is
Plane

        } ?: return null

        return
hitResult.createAnchor()

    }

}
```

4. Using MQTT for Real-Time Communication

For direct communication, MQTT is a popular protocol for IoT.

MQTT Client Setup

kotlin

```
val          mqttClient          =
MqttClient("tcp://broker.hive
mq.com:1883",
MqttClient.generateClientId()
, null)

mqttClient.connect()

mqttClient.subscribe("iot/sen
sor")


mqttClient.setCallback(object
: MqttCallback {
```

```kotlin
    override                fun
messageArrived(topic:
String?,              message:
MqttMessage?) {

        val    payload    =
message?.payload?.toString(Ch
arsets.UTF_8)

        val    sensorData    =
Gson().fromJson(payload,
SensorData::class.java)


updateArOverlay(sensorData)

    }


    override                fun
connectionLost(cause:
Throwable?) {}
```

```
override                    fun
deliveryComplete(token:
IMqttDeliveryToken?) {}

})
```

Testing and Debugging

1. **Test API Calls**: Use tools like Postman to verify the API's response.
2. **Check AR Alignment**: Ensure AR overlays are positioned accurately relative to real-world objects.
3. **Network Latency**: Minimize delays in data fetching or MQTT communication.

Best Practices for AR and IoT Integration

1. **Optimize Data Updates**: Avoid overloading the network with frequent requests.
2. **Secure Communication**: Use HTTPS for APIs and MQTT over TLS for secure data transmission.
3. **Provide Feedback**: Display loading indicators if data retrieval is delayed.

6.5 Performance Optimization: Reducing Latency and Improving User Experience

Performance optimization is crucial for AR applications to deliver a seamless and engaging user experience. By focusing on reducing latency and ensuring smooth interactions, you can make your app feel responsive and immersive, even on resource-constrained devices.

This chapter delves into the techniques and tools you can use to optimize your AR app for performance, ensuring a balance between graphical fidelity, real-time responsiveness, and user satisfaction.

Understanding Performance Challenges in AR

1. **Rendering Latency**: Delays in rendering can cause mismatches between the AR object and the real-world environment.
2. **Resource Constraints**: AR applications are computationally intensive, requiring efficient CPU and GPU utilization.
3. **Data Latency**: Real-time interactions, such as fetching IoT data or handling gestures, must occur without noticeable lag.
4. **Battery Drain**: Intensive computation and sensors like the camera can quickly deplete battery life.

1. Optimizing Graphics Rendering

Graphics rendering is one of the most resource-intensive aspects of AR applications. To optimize rendering:

a. Reduce Draw Calls

Minimize the number of objects rendered per frame. Batch renderable objects when possible:

kotlin

```
// Example: Reusing a single
renderable    for    multiple
objects

private                    fun
createOptimizedNode(renderabl
e: ModelRenderable, position:
Vector3): Node {
```

```
val node = Node()

node.renderable        =
renderable

node.localPosition     =
position

return node
}
```

b. Use Simplified Models

Replace high-polygon 3D models with optimized, low-polygon versions without sacrificing visual quality. Tools like Blender or Unity's mesh simplification can help.

c. Enable Frame Throttling

Reduce the target frame rate on less powerful devices to ensure smoother performance:

kotlin

```kotlin
arFragment.arSceneView.scene?
.frameRate = FrameRate.LOW
```

---

2. Reducing Latency

Latency directly affects user experience in AR. Here's how to reduce it:

a. Asynchronous Data Fetching

Fetch data in the background to prevent blocking the main UI thread:

kotlin

```kotlin
CoroutineScope(Dispatchers.IO
).launch {
```

```kotlin
    val data =
api.getSensorData()            //
Network call

withContext(Dispatchers.Main)
{
        updateUI(data)         //
Update UI after fetching data
    }
}
```

b. Preloading Resources

Load 3D models, textures, and assets in advance to prevent delays during runtime:

kotlin

```
ModelRenderable.builder()
```

```
    .setSource(this,
Uri.parse("optimized_model.gl
b"))

    .build()

    .thenAccept              {
modelRenderable ->

        renderable        =
modelRenderable

    }
```

---

3. Managing CPU and GPU Usage

Efficient resource management ensures your app runs smoothly:

a. Optimize Scene Complexity

Limit the number of objects and effects in the AR scene. Use occlusion sparingly and only when it adds significant value.

b. Adjust Lighting

Dynamic lighting is computationally expensive. Opt for baked lighting or simple ambient lighting for static objects:

kotlin

```
Light.builder(Light.Type.DIRE
CTIONAL)

    .setColor(Color(1f,    1f,
1f)) // White light

    .setIntensity(0.5f)    //
Moderate brightness

    .build()
```

4. Memory Management

AR apps can quickly consume memory, leading to crashes or degraded performance.

a. Use Object Pooling

Reuse objects instead of creating new ones:

kotlin

```
val        objectPool      =
ArrayDeque<Node>()


fun getPooledObject(): Node {
    return              if
(objectPool.isNotEmpty()) {
```

```
objectPool.removeFirst()

    } else {

        Node() // Create new
object if pool is empty

    }

}


fun releaseObject(node: Node)
{

    objectPool.addLast(node)

}
```

b. Dispose of Unused Resources

Release memory by clearing unused objects and assets:

kotlin

```kotlin
override fun onDestroy() {

    super.onDestroy()

    renderable?.let {

        it.destroy()

        renderable = null

    }

}
```

---

5. Improving User Experience

Optimizing performance is not just about technical improvements; it's also about how users perceive the app.

a. Provide Feedback for Long Operations

Use loading indicators or animations while fetching data:

kotlin

```
progressBar.visibility         =
View.VISIBLE

CoroutineScope(Dispatchers.IO
).launch {

    val data = fetchData()


withContext(Dispatchers.Main)
{


progressBar.visibility         =
View.GONE

        displayData(data)
```

```
        }

}
```

b. Use Adaptive Graphics Settings

Allow users to choose performance or quality modes:

kotlin

```
fun        setGraphicsMode(mode:
String) {

    when (mode) {

        "performance"        ->
arFragment.arSceneView.scene?
.frameRate = FrameRate.LOW

        "quality"        ->
arFragment.arSceneView.scene?
.frameRate = FrameRate.HIGH
```

```
        }

}
```

6. Tools for Performance Optimization

1. **Android Profiler**: Monitor CPU, memory, and network usage in real-time.
2. **ARCore Performance Hints**: ARCore provides hints about performance bottlenecks.
3. **Unity or Unreal Engine**: If your app is highly graphical, consider leveraging engines with built-in optimizations.

Sample Optimization Workflow

Let's apply some of these techniques to optimize an AR app.

Scenario: Placing multiple 3D objects in AR with real-time data updates.

Step 1: Reduce Scene Complexity

- Combine static models into a single mesh.
- Preload assets before starting the AR session.

Step 2: Optimize Data Fetching

Use coroutines to fetch data asynchronously while maintaining responsiveness.

Step 3: Implement Memory Management

Pool frequently used objects, such as labels or markers.

Code Example

kotlin

```
CoroutineScope(Dispatchers.IO
).launch {
```

```kotlin
    val     sensorData    =
api.getSensorData()

withContext(Dispatchers.Main)
{

        updateUI(sensorData)

    }

}


// Preload assets

ModelRenderable.builder()

    .setSource(this,
Uri.parse("model.glb"))

    .build()

    .thenAccept { renderable
->
```

```
        //   Store    renderable
for reuse

    }
```

By reducing latency, managing resources efficiently, and considering user experience, you can create AR apps that perform well across various devices. Optimization is an iterative process, and regular profiling and testing are key to achieving a polished experience.

Hands-On Project: Create a Basic AR Game with Object Interactions and Scoring

In this hands-on project, we'll build a simple augmented reality (AR) game using Kotlin and ARCore. The game will allow players to interact with objects in an AR environment, track their actions, and maintain a score. This project will reinforce the concepts of object placement, user interaction, and performance optimization.

Project Overview

Objective

Create an AR-based game where users "catch" objects as they appear in the AR scene. Each successful interaction increases their score.

Features

- AR object placement at random positions.
- Gesture-based interaction (tap to "catch" objects).
- Real-time score tracking and display.

Requirements

1. Android Studio (latest version recommended).
2. ARCore SDK integrated into your project.
3. Basic Kotlin programming knowledge.

Step 1: Setting Up the Project

Create a New Project

1. Open Android Studio and create a new project with the following settings:
   - **Template**: Empty Activity.
   - **Language**: Kotlin.
   - **Minimum SDK**: API Level 24 or higher.
2. Add ARCore dependencies to your `build.gradle` file:

gradle

```
dependencies {

    implementation
'com.google.ar:core:1.38.0'

    implementation
'com.google.ar.sceneform:core
:1.10.0'
```

```
}
```

3. Sync the project.

Step 2: Initializing the AR Scene

Update the Layout

Modify `activity_main.xml` to include an ARFragment for rendering AR content:

xml

```
<androidx.fragment.app.Fragme
ntContainerView


android:id="@+id/ar_fragment"
```

```
android:name="com.google.ar.s
ceneform.ux.ArFragment"

android:layout_width="match_p
arent"

android:layout_height="match_
parent" />

<TextView

android:id="@+id/score_text"

android:layout_width="wrap_co
ntent"
```

```
android:layout_height="wrap_c
ontent"

android:layout_margin="16dp"

    android:text="Score: 0"

    android:textSize="24sp"

android:textColor="#FFFFFF"

android:background="#88000000
"

    android:padding="8dp"

android:layout_alignParentTop
="true"
```

```
android:layout_alignParentSta
rt="true" />
```

Initialize AR in MainActivity

Set up the AR scene and add a listener for tap gestures:

kotlin

```
class        MainActivity        :
AppCompatActivity() {

    private     lateinit     var
arFragment: ArFragment

    private var score = 0
```

```kotlin
    override                fun
onCreate(savedInstanceState:
Bundle?) {

super.onCreate(savedInstanceS
tate)

setContentView(R.layout.activ
ity_main)


    arFragment          =
supportFragmentManager.findFr
agmentById(R.id.ar_fragment)
as ArFragment


    // Initialize   tap
listener
```

```kotlin
arFragment.setOnTapArPlaneLis
tener { hitResult, _, _ ->


placeRandomObject(hitResult.c
reateAnchor())

        }

    }


    private                    fun
placeRandomObject(anchor:
Anchor) {


ModelRenderable.builder()

        .setSource(this,
Uri.parse("object.glb"))     //
Replace with your 3D model
```

```
        .build()

            .thenAccept        {
renderable ->

                val
anchorNode                        =
AnchorNode(anchor)


anchorNode.setParent(arFragme
nt.arSceneView.scene)


                val
objectNode                        =
TransformableNode(arFragment.
transformationSystem)


objectNode.renderable        =
renderable
```

```kotlin
        objectNode.setParent(anchorNo
de)

        objectNode.setOnTapListener  {
_, _ ->

                      score++

updateScore()

anchorNode.setParent(null)  //
Remove object
                }
            }
        }
```

```
private fun updateScore()
{

findViewById<TextView>(R.id.s
core_text).text   =   "Score:
$score"

    }

}
```

Step 3: Adding Randomized Object Placement

Objects should appear at random positions within the AR scene to increase engagement.

Modify Object Placement

Enhance the `placeRandomObject` method to position objects randomly:

kotlin

```
private                       fun
placeRandomObject(anchor:
Anchor) {

    ModelRenderable.builder()

        .setSource(this,
Uri.parse("object.glb"))

        .build()

        .thenAccept          {
renderable ->

            val anchorNode   =
AnchorNode(anchor)
```

```kotlin
anchorNode.setParent(arFragme
nt.arSceneView.scene)


        val objectNode =
TransformableNode(arFragment.
transformationSystem)


objectNode.renderable         =
renderable


        //    Set    random
position
        val
randomPosition = Vector3(

(Math.random()    *    2    -
1).toFloat(), // Random X
```

```kotlin
            (Math.random()    *    0.5    +
0.5).toFloat(), // Random Y


            (Math.random()         *         -
2).toFloat() // Random Z

                    )


        objectNode.localPosition       =
randomPosition



        objectNode.setParent(anchorNo
de)


        objectNode.setOnTapListener  {
_, _ ->
                    score++
```

```kotlin
                    updateScore()


anchorNode.setParent(null)   //
Remove object

                    }

          }

}
```

Step 4: Tracking and Displaying the Score

The `updateScore` method already updates the score in real time. Let's ensure it refreshes the display efficiently:

kotlin

```kotlin
private fun updateScore() {

    runOnUiThread {

        findViewById<TextView>(R.id.score_text).text = "Score: $score"

    }

}
```

Step 5: Enhancing the Game

a. Timer for Game Duration

Add a timer to make the game more challenging:

kotlin

```kotlin
private var timeLeft = 30 // 30 seconds


private fun startTimer() {
    val timer = object :
CountDownTimer(30000, 1000) {

        override fun
onTick(millisUntilFinished:
Long) {

            timeLeft--


findViewById<TextView>(R.id.s
core_text).text = "Time:
$timeLeft | Score: $score"

        }
```

```kotlin
        override            fun
onFinish() {

Toast.makeText(this@MainActiv
ity, "Game Over! Final Score:
$score",
Toast.LENGTH_LONG).show()

            }

        }

    timer.start()

}
```

Call startTimer() in onCreate.

b. Increasing Difficulty

Make objects disappear if not tapped within
a few seconds:

kotlin

```kotlin
private                    fun
placeRandomObject(anchor:
Anchor) {

    // Previous code ...



objectNode.setOnTapListener {
_, _ ->

        score++

        updateScore()

anchorNode.setParent(null) //
Remove object

    }
```

```
Handler(Looper.getMainLooper(
)).postDelayed({

        if  (anchorNode.parent
!= null) {


anchorNode.setParent(null)   //
Remove after delay

        }

    }, 3000) // 3 seconds

}
```

Step 6: Testing and Debugging

1. **Debugging Object Placement**:
   - Ensure objects appear within the camera view.
   - Use logs to verify random position calculations.
2. **Testing User Interactions**:
   - Confirm taps register correctly.
   - Check the score updates as expected.
3. **Performance Testing**:
   - Test on multiple devices for smooth rendering.
   - Profile memory usage to avoid crashes.

Conclusion

This chapter provided a comprehensive overview of advanced AR features in Kotlin, equipping you to build interactive and high-performance AR apps. The hands-on project showcased how to create a fun and engaging

AR game, blending creativity with technical skills. Keep experimenting and pushing the boundaries of what your AR apps can do!

Chapter 7: AR User Interface Design

AR user interface (UI) design merges virtual elements with real-world contexts, ensuring intuitive and engaging interactions. In this chapter, we'll explore how to craft AR UIs using Kotlin, Jetpack Compose, and ARCore. We'll cover everything from creating menus and controls to best practices for navigation and accessibility.

7.1 Designing AR Interfaces with Kotlin and Jetpack Compose

Overview

Jetpack Compose simplifies UI development with a declarative approach. Using Compose for AR apps enables seamless integration of dynamic UI components into the AR experience.

549

Example: Overlaying a Scoreboard

Let's add a dynamic scoreboard UI using Jetpack Compose.

Step 1: Add Compose Dependencies

Update your `build.gradle`:

gradle

```gradle
dependencies {

    implementation
"androidx.compose.ui:ui:1.4.0
"

    implementation
"androidx.compose.material:ma
terial:1.4.0"

    implementation
"androidx.compose.ui:ui-
tooling:1.4.0"
```

```
    implementation
"androidx.lifecycle:lifecycle
-runtime-ktx:2.6.1"

}
```

Enable Compose in your project:

gradle

```
android {

    buildFeatures {

        compose true

    }

    composeOptions {

kotlinCompilerExtensionVersio
n '1.4.0'
```

```
        }

    }
```

Step 2: Define the Scoreboard UI

Create a Compose function for the scoreboard:

kotlin

```
@Composable

fun   Scoreboard(score:      Int,
timeLeft: Int) {

     Column(

         modifier = Modifier

             .fillMaxWidth()

             .padding(16.dp)
```

```
.background(Color(0x88000000)
, RoundedCornerShape(8.dp))
                .padding(16.dp)
    ) {
        Text(
            text    =    "Score:
$score",
            color              =
Color.White,
            fontSize = 20.sp
        )
        Text(
            text    =    "Time
Left: $timeLeft sec",
```

```
            color              =
Color.White,

            fontSize = 16.sp

        )

    }

}
```

Step 3: Integrate Compose UI in MainActivity

Wrap the AR scene with Compose UI:

kotlin

```
class        MainActivity      :
ComponentActivity() {

    private   var    score    by
mutableStateOf(0)
```

```kotlin
    private var timeLeft by
mutableStateOf(30)


    override               fun
onCreate(savedInstanceState:
Bundle?) {


super.onCreate(savedInstanceS
tate)

        setContent {

            Box(modifier      =
Modifier.fillMaxSize()) {

                AndroidView(

                    factory =
{ ArFragment().view },

                    modifier
= Modifier.fillMaxSize()
```

```kotlin
        )

        Scoreboard(score    =    score,
        timeLeft = timeLeft)

                }

        }


        //        Example        of
updating score and timer

Handler(Looper.getMainLooper(
)).postDelayed({
            score += 10

            timeLeft -= 5

        }, 5000)

    }
```

```
}
```

7.2 Creating AR Menus and Controls: Interaction Design

Menus in AR apps provide intuitive ways to access settings, tools, or information. These can be implemented using Compose overlays or directly in the AR scene.

Example: Adding an AR Menu

Step 1: Define the Menu

Create a vertical menu for options:

kotlin

```
@Composable

fun   ARMenu(onOptionSelected:
(String) -> Unit) {
```

```kotlin
Column(
    modifier = Modifier
        .fillMaxWidth()

        .wrapContentHeight()

        .background(Color(0xCC000000)
)
        .padding(8.dp)
) {
    listOf("Restart",
"Settings", "Exit").forEach {
option ->
        Button(
            onClick = {
onOptionSelected(option) },
```

```
                    modifier        =
Modifier

.fillMaxWidth()

.padding(4.dp)

           ) {

                    Text(text      =
option,  color  =  Color.White)

           }

       }

    }

}
```

Step 2: Integrate Menu with Actions

Call the menu in your UI and handle interactions:

kotlin

```
setContent {

    var selectedOption by
remember { mutableStateOf("")
}


    Box(modifier          =
Modifier.fillMaxSize()) {

        ARMenu { option ->

            selectedOption =
option

            when (option) {
```

```
                "Restart"    ->
restartGame()

                "Settings"   ->
openSettings()

                "Exit"       ->
finish()

            }

        }

    }

}
```

7.3 Best Practices for AR App Layouts and Navigation

1. **Minimal UI**: Keep the UI non-intrusive to avoid blocking the AR view.
2. **Accessible Placement**: Position elements where users can easily reach them without disrupting the AR experience.
3. **Feedback and Cues**: Provide clear feedback for interactions using sound, animation, or haptic responses.

7.4 Making Your AR App Accessible

Voice Commands

Use Google's Speech API to add voice input for hands-free interaction.

Example

kotlin

```kotlin
private                    fun
startVoiceRecognition() {

    val        intent         =
Intent(RecognizerIntent.ACTIO
N_RECOGNIZE_SPEECH)


intent.putExtra(RecognizerInt
ent.EXTRA_LANGUAGE_MODEL,
RecognizerIntent.LANGUAGE_MOD
EL_FREE_FORM)


startActivityForResult(intent
, VOICE_REQUEST_CODE)

}


override                    fun
onActivityResult(requestCode:
```

```kotlin
Int, resultCode: Int, data:
Intent?) {

super.onActivityResult(reques
tCode, resultCode, data)
    if (requestCode ==
VOICE_REQUEST_CODE &&
resultCode == RESULT_OK) {

        val results =
data?.getStringArrayListExtra
(RecognizerIntent.EXTRA_RESUL
TS)

        val command =
results?.get(0)

handleVoiceCommand(command)
    }
}
```

7.5 Testing AR Interfaces with Users

Testing Checklist

1. **Usability Testing**: Ensure users can intuitively navigate the app.
2. **Stress Testing**: Simulate real-world conditions like varied lighting.
3. **Accessibility Testing**: Verify compatibility with screen readers and voice commands.

Hands-On Project: Build an AR App with a Customizable Menu and Interactive Buttons

Overview

We'll design an AR app with a menu that allows users to add objects, reset the scene, and exit the app.

Step-by-Step Guide

1. **Setup Project**:
   - Follow previous steps to create an AR app.
   - Use Jetpack Compose for UI elements.

Add Menu Options: Define menu actions such as *Add Object*, *Reset Scene*, and *Exit*: kotlin

```kotlin
@Composable

fun
ARGameMenu(onOptionSelected:
(String) -> Unit) {

    val options = listOf("Add
Object", "Reset", "Exit")

    Column {

        options.forEach         {
option ->
```

```kotlin
            Button(onClick    =
{ onOptionSelected(option) })
{

            Text(option)

        }

    }

}

}
```

Handle Menu Actions: Implement logic for each menu action: kotlin

```kotlin
when (selectedOption) {

    "Add      Object"      ->
addARObject()

    "Reset" -> resetScene()
```

```
"Exit" -> finish()

}
```

2.

3. **Enhance User Experience**: Add
   animations, transitions, or haptic
   feedback for interactions.

This chapter has demonstrated how to
integrate AR-specific UI elements using
Kotlin and Jetpack Compose. By combining
clear menus, accessible inputs, and
thoughtful layout practices, you can create
AR experiences that feel both intuitive and
engaging. Continue experimenting with
these tools to refine your app's user
experience further.

Chapter 8: Deploying Your AR App

Creating an AR app is only part of the journey; deploying it to the Google Play Store ensures it reaches users. This chapter walks you through testing, debugging, preparing, and publishing your AR app. By the end, you'll have the tools and knowledge to successfully launch your AR app and monitor its performance post-launch.

8.1 Preparing for Google Play Store Deployment

Step 1: Create a Developer Account

1. Visit the Google Play Console and sign up as a developer.
2. Pay the one-time registration fee.
3. Fill out the required details, including payment and tax information.

Step 2: Check Play Store Requirements

Ensure your app meets the following:

- **Privacy Policy**: Link to your privacy policy.
- **App Name & Description**: Create concise, engaging text.
- **App Icon**: Use a 512x512 PNG with transparency.
- **Screenshots**: Minimum two, showcasing your app in action.
- **Feature Graphic**: A 1024x500 PNG that highlights your app's purpose.

8.2 Testing Your AR App on Real Devices

Testing on actual devices is critical for identifying real-world issues.

Step 1: Connect and Deploy

1. Connect your device via USB or Wi-Fi.

2. Enable **Developer Options** and **USB Debugging** on your device:
   ○ Go to **Settings** > **About Phone**.
   ○ Tap **Build Number** seven times to enable Developer Options.
   ○ Navigate to **Developer Options** > Enable **USB Debugging**.
3. Deploy the app from Android Studio:
   ○ Click **Run** ▶□ in Android Studio.
   ○ Select your device in the target dialog.

Step 2: Verify AR Functionality

- Check AR object placement and tracking.
- Test performance under varying lighting and environments.
- Validate user interactions (e.g., gestures and touch inputs).

8.3 Debugging Common Issues in AR Apps

Issue 1: ARCore Not Installed

Ensure ARCore is installed on the test device. Include a prompt in your app:

kotlin

```
val availability = ArCoreApk.getInstance().checkAvailability(this)

if (availability.isTransient) {

    // Show a dialog or notification to inform users

}
```

Issue 2: Poor Tracking Performance

- Ensure the AR session is correctly configured with environmental settings:

kotlin

```
config.lightEstimationMode   =
Config.LightEstimationMode.EN
VIRONMENTAL_HDR

config.planeFindingMode      =
Config.PlaneFindingMode.HORIZ
ONTAL_AND_VERTICAL
```

Issue 3: App Crashes on Startup

1. Check for unhandled exceptions in **Logcat**.
2. Ensure permissions for the camera are granted:

kotlin

```kotlin
if
(ContextCompat.checkSelfPermi
ssion(this,
Manifest.permission.CAMERA)
!=
PackageManager.PERMISSION_GRA
NTED) {


ActivityCompat.requestPermiss
ions(this,
arrayOf(Manifest.permission.C
AMERA),
CAMERA_PERMISSION_REQUEST_COD
E)

}
```

8.4 Packaging Your App for the Store

Step 1: Generate a Signed APK

1. Open **Build** > **Generate Signed Bundle/APK**.
2. Select **APK** > **Next**.
3. Create or use an existing keystore:
   - Provide a secure password.
   - Save the keystore file securely (it's required for future updates).
4. Choose a **release build** and finish the process.

Step 2: Enable ProGuard for Code Shrinking

Add the following in your build.gradle:

gradle

```
buildTypes {

    release {

        minifyEnabled true

        proguardFiles
getDefaultProguardFile('progu
ard-android-optimize.txt'),
'proguard-rules.pro'

    }

}
```

8.5 Post-Deployment: Gathering Feedback and User Engagement

Step 1: Integrate Analytics

Use Firebase Analytics to monitor user interactions:

1. Add Firebase to your project:
   ○ Go to Firebase Console.
   ○ Add your app by downloading the `google-services.json` file.

Add the dependency:
gradle

```
implementation
'com.google.firebase:firebase
-analytics-ktx:21.3.0'
```

2.

Log events:
kotlin

```
val firebaseAnalytics =
Firebase.analytics

firebaseAnalytics.logEvent(Fi
rebaseAnalytics.Event.SELECT_
CONTENT) {
```

```
param(FirebaseAnalytics.Param
.ITEM_ID, "AR_Object")


param(FirebaseAnalytics.Param
.CONTENT_TYPE, "interaction")

}
```

Step 2: Respond to Feedback

- Regularly check the Google Play
  Console for user reviews.
- Update your app to address reported
  issues.

Hands-On Project: Publish Your AR App to Google Play Store and Monitor Analytics

Step-by-Step Instructions

Step 1: Prepare Your App

1. Test thoroughly on multiple devices.
2. Optimize graphics and AR performance.
3. Ensure your app icon, screenshots, and feature graphic are ready.

Step 2: Upload to Google Play Console

1. Log in to Google Play Console.
2. Create a new app:
   - Enter the app name, language, and default details.
   - Select **Free** or **Paid**.
3. Upload the signed APK or App Bundle.

Step 3: Fill Out Store Details

- **App Content**: Enter privacy policy, content rating, and app classification.
- **Pricing & Distribution**: Set pricing and available regions.
- **Release**: Publish to a testing track first (internal, closed, or open testing).

Step 4: Monitor Analytics

After release, monitor user activity using Firebase:

- Track installs, uninstalls, and active users.
- Observe interaction patterns with AR features.

Step 5: Update and Maintain

- Release regular updates with bug fixes and new features.
- Maintain responsiveness to user feedback.

By following these steps, you'll successfully deploy your AR app and ensure its performance aligns with user expectations. A good deployment strategy, combined with effective post-launch monitoring, can significantly enhance user satisfaction and app longevity.

Chapter 9: Future of AR with Kotlin and Android

Augmented Reality (AR) is transforming industries, reshaping experiences, and redefining how users interact with the digital world. In this chapter, we'll explore the future of AR, the role Kotlin plays in its evolution, emerging trends, and how you can stay ahead in this rapidly growing field.

9.1 The Growth of Augmented Reality and Its Future Applications

The Current Landscape

AR technology has progressed from novelty to necessity in various sectors:

- **Healthcare**: Surgical training and real-time medical imaging.
- **Retail**: Virtual try-ons and immersive shopping experiences.

- **Education**: Interactive learning through AR-enhanced content.
- **Gaming**: Games like *Pokémon GO* have demonstrated AR's potential for immersive entertainment.

Future Applications

1. **AR in Smart Cities**: Navigation, infrastructure visualization, and public safety enhancements.
2. **Industrial Use Cases**: Maintenance, prototyping, and assembly line support through AR overlays.
3. **Personalized AR**: Tailoring AR experiences based on user preferences and behaviors.

9.2 Emerging Trends in AR: AR Cloud, 5G, and Beyond

1. AR Cloud

The AR Cloud allows for persistent AR experiences by syncing digital content with the physical world. It enables:

- Multi-user AR experiences.
- Location-based AR interactions that remain consistent across devices.

2. The Role of 5G

5G enhances AR with:

- Low latency for real-time interactions.
- High bandwidth for streaming high-quality AR content.

3. Artificial Intelligence (AI) and AR

AI algorithms enhance AR by:

- Improving object recognition.

- Generating realistic 3D models dynamically.

4. Hardware Advances

- **AR Glasses**: Devices like the Magic Leap and HoloLens are shaping the hardware future.
- **Wearable AR**: AR integrated with smartwatches and other wearables.

9.3 Kotlin's Role in the Evolving AR Landscape

Kotlin is a modern, robust language that complements AR development:

- **Efficiency**: Kotlin's concise syntax allows developers to focus on complex AR logic.
- **Interoperability**: Kotlin works seamlessly with existing Java-based libraries, including ARCore.

- **Coroutines**: Kotlin Coroutines handle real-time data streams and processing in AR applications efficiently.

Kotlin continues to evolve, integrating new libraries and frameworks that enhance its capability for AR app development.

9.4 Resources for Continued Learning:

To remain proficient in AR development, it's vital to stay updated with the latest trends and tools. Here are resources to help you continue learning:

Online Communities

- **Stack Overflow**: Engage with the Kotlin and AR development community.
- **Kotlin Slack**: Participate in discussions on Kotlin-specific use cases.

Courses and Tutorials

- **Udemy and Coursera**: AR development courses.
- **Google Developers Training**: Official Kotlin and Android tutorials.

Blogs and Publications

- **Google's AR Blog**: Latest ARCore updates and use cases.
- **Kotlin Blog**: Updates on language features and libraries.

Conferences

- **Google I/O**: Sessions on ARCore and Kotlin.
- **AR/VR Developer Conferences**: Focus on cutting-edge AR trends.

587

Assessment

Brainstorm and Plan an Innovative AR App Idea Based on Future Trends

This project encourages creativity and strategic thinking by leveraging future AR trends.

Step 1: Identify a Problem

Step 2: Map the App Features

Step 3: Sketch Your Idea

Step 4: Choose Your Technology Stack

Step 5: Evaluate Feasibility

Assess:

- Hardware requirements (AR-compatible devices).
- Potential challenges (e.g., poor lighting conditions for object detection).

Conclusion

The future of AR with Kotlin and Android is limitless. As AR technology advances, it will unlock new possibilities for immersive experiences. By leveraging Kotlin's modern capabilities and staying informed about emerging trends, you can create innovative AR applications that shape the future. This chapter has equipped you with the knowledge and inspiration to take AR development to the next level—now it's your turn to imagine, design, and build the AR experiences of tomorrow.

Appendices

The appendices serve as a quick-reference section, designed to support your AR development journey with essential Kotlin syntax, ARCore API details, solutions to common issues, and key AR terminology. Whether you're a beginner or an experienced developer, these resources will be invaluable.

A. Kotlin Reference Cheat Sheet

Here's a concise reference for essential Kotlin syntax and concepts:

Basics
kotlin

```
// Variable Declaration
val immutableValue: String =
"Hello, Kotlin!" // Immutable
```

```kotlin
var mutableValue: Int = 10 //
Mutable

// Functions
fun    greet(name:    String):
String {
    return "Hello, $name!"
}

// Single-Expression Function
fun add(a: Int, b: Int) = a +
b

// Null Safety
var nullableString: String? =
null
nullableString?.let          {
println(it)  }  //  Executes
only if not null
```

Control Structures
kotlin

```kotlin
// If-Else
val max = if (a > b) a else b

// When
val dayType = when (day) {
    "Saturday", "Sunday" -> "Weekend"
    else -> "Weekday"
}

// Loops
for (i in 1..5) println(i) // Inclusive range
while (x > 0) x--
```

Collections
kotlin

```kotlin
val numbers = listOf(1, 2, 3)
// Immutable List
val mutableNumbers =
mutableListOf(1, 2, 3)

mutableNumbers.add(4) // [1,
2, 3, 4]
```

Classes and Objects
kotlin

```kotlin
class Person(val name:
String, var age: Int)

val person = Person("Alice",
25)
println(person.name) // Alice
```

This cheat sheet highlights Kotlin's simplicity and expressiveness—essential for AR app development.

B. ARCore API Reference

ARCore provides a robust set of tools for creating AR experiences. Here are the most used APIs:

Session Management

- `ArSession`: Manages the AR environment.
- **Example**:

kotlin

```
val session = Session(context)
val config = Config(session)
config.updateMode = Config.UpdateMode.LATEST_CAMERA_IMAGE
session.configure(config)
```

Planes

- Detect and interact with flat surfaces.
- **Key Methods**:
  - ```
    session.getAllTrackab
    les(Plane::class.java
    )
    ```
  - ```
    plane.isPoseInPolygon
    (pose)
    ```

Anchors

- Anchor virtual objects to the real world.
- **Example**:

kotlin

```
val          anchor         =
hitResult.createAnchor()
val          anchorNode     =
AnchorNode(anchor).apply     {
```

```kotlin
setParent(arFragment.arSceneV
iew.scene) }
```

Augmented Images

- Recognize images and overlay AR content.
- **Configuration**:

kotlin

```kotlin
config.augmentedImageDatabase
=
AugmentedImageDatabase(sessio
n)
```

C. Troubleshooting Common Issues in AR Development

1. Poor Plane Detection

- **Symptoms**: Planes are not detected or take too long to appear.

- **Solution**:
  - Ensure sufficient lighting.
  - Avoid reflective or featureless surfaces.

2. Objects Drifting

- **Symptoms**: Anchored objects move from their original positions.
- **Solution**:
  - Use `ARSession.update()` to refresh tracking.
  - Limit the number of active anchors.

3. App Crashes on Startup

- **Symptoms**: The app crashes immediately after launch.
- **Solution**:
  - Verify ARCore installation.
  - Ensure `minSdkVersion` is set to 24 or higher in `build.gradle`.

4. Performance Lag

- **Symptoms**: The app responds slowly or freezes.
- **Solution**:
  - Optimize 3D assets for fewer polygons.
  - Use `Config.LightEstimatio nMode.DISABLED` if lighting is not critical.

Debugging Tips

- Use `Logcat` in Android Studio to trace errors.
- Utilize `try-catch` blocks to capture runtime exceptions.

D. Glossary of Terms

1. Anchor

A fixed point in the real world where AR objects are placed.

2. ARCore

Google's SDK for building AR applications on Android.

3. Augmented Reality (AR)

A technology that overlays virtual content on the real world.

4. Pose

Represents the position and orientation of an object in 3D space.

5. Raycasting

The process of sending an invisible ray into the AR environment to detect surfaces or objects.

6. Sceneform

A high-level library for rendering 3D objects in AR applications.

7. SLAM (Simultaneous Localization and Mapping)

A technique used by ARCore to map environments and track user positions.

8. Tracking

The process of understanding the device's position relative to the world.

9. World-Space

A 3D coordinate system that ARCore uses to position objects in the real world.

The appendices provide quick access to vital information, from Kotlin syntax and ARCore APIs to troubleshooting tips and industry terminology. These resources ensure you're well-equipped to tackle any AR development challenge, regardless of your skill level.

www.ingramcontent.com/pod-product-compliance
Lightning Source LLC
LaVergne TN
LVHW022332060326
832902LV00022B/3991